Echoes of the Ancient World

Series editor Werner Forman

IN THE SHADOW
OF THE PYRAMIDS

IN THE SHADOW OF THE PYRAMIDS

Egypt during the Old Kingdom

Text by Jaromir Malek

Photographs by Werner Forman

University of Oklahoma Press
Norman, Oklahoma

To J.J. and P. with love

*But the iniquity of oblivion blindely scattereth her poppy, and deals with the
memory of men without distinction to merit of perpetuity. Who can but
pity the founder of the Pyramids?*
(Sir Thomas Browne, *Hydriotaphia,* 1658)

Note on the rendering of ancient Egyptian words:

As in many cases we do not know with certainty how ancient Egyptian
words were pronounced, they are given—with one or two exceptions—
in the standarized form used by Egyptologists. The same applies to
royal and private names. For one of the kings of the Fourth Dynasty
I have, however, preferred the non-committal Greek form Khephren
because the correct reading is still a matter of dispute.

*Half-title page: Relief-decoration could be equally well applied to a wooden surface, in this
case a stela (false-door), as to stone. The couple represented here are Iyka, a 'manager of
the royal estate'* (**hut–aat**) *and 'royal priest', and his wife Iymert.*

*Title page: The familiar silhouettes of the pyramids of Khufu, Khephren and Menkaure at
Giza, to the south-west of modern Cairo.*

*Front cover: The pyramid of Khufu at Giza, the largest in Egypt, partly obscured by the
pyramid of Khephren. Back cover: The pyramid of Khephran at Giza, showing the
exposed filling blocks covering the core of the structure. The original casing blocks are still
preserved at the base and near the summit.*

Copyright © Little Brown and Company (UK) Ltd.
Photographs copyright © Werner Forman 1986
First published in Great Britain 1986 by Orbis Book Publishing Corporation Limited, London
Published in the United States by University of Oklahoma Pres, Norman, Publishing Division of the University
First edition 1986
Printed in Italy by New Interlitho

2 3 4 5 6 7 8 9 10 11 12 13 14 15 16 17

Library of Congress Cataloging-in-Publication Data

Málek, Jaromír
In the shadow of the pyramids

I. Egypt—Civilization—To 332b.c. I. Forman, W (Werner) III. Title.
DTM M29 1986   932′.012   86–40188
ISBN 0–8061–2027–1 (Paper)
ISBN 0–8061–2029–0 (Cloth)

CONTENTS

ONE

PROLOGUE

MANETHO, AN EGYPTIAN PRIEST living under the Ptolemies Soter and Philadelphus, compiled a history of Egypt based on old records and archive lists of kings. History-writing was a concept alien to Egyptian thinking, and although his was a good native name (*manehto*, 'horse-groom') and his origins from an important provincial town of Sebennytos in the central Delta were beyond reproach, it was a foreign culture and an un-Egyptian world outlook which inspired the work. Manetho's *Aigyptiaka* was written in Greek and has come down to us only in the form of excerpts made from it by later chroniclers, but it has exerted a lasting effect on the formal division of the political history of ancient Egypt and the way it is traditionally interpreted.

Following the usage of his time, Manetho divided the kings known to him into thirty dynasties or ruling houses, starting with the legendary Menes and concluding with the last native king, Nektanebos. Some of these divisions followed ancient king-lists, others seem to have resulted from his misunderstanding of the sources, or their imperfection, and several may have been introduced by him simply for convenience. Nevertheless, Manetho's dynastic division is still generally used and its author is deservedly regarded as the first Egyptian historian.

The ancient Egyptians did not record history for its own sake and our knowledge is, therefore, based on history's raw materials and on texts which were composed for other purposes. Yet the Egyptians were not entirely oblivious of their past. A rare insight into their awareness of it is still visible in a large memorial temple built by King Seti I for the perpetuation of his cult in the Upper Egyptian town of Abdju (Abydos) a thousand years before Manetho, around 1300 BC. In the maze of its chapels, columned halls, and vestibules there is a corridor known as 'The Gallery of the Lists.' In the relief carved on its east wall Seti I and his son, the future Ramesse II, are shown symbolically offering libation and incense to a large number of Egyptian deities represented by their names. On the opposite west wall the father and son appear in a similar scene before two long rows of cartouches containing the names of their royal ancestors. The list, by its nature, did not aspire to historical completeness.

The remarkable accuracy of pyramid construction and the mathematical properties of the design, which may sometimes involve the use of π (e.g. the height of the pyramid of Khufu $= \dfrac{\text{perimeter of the base}}{2\pi}$), can be rationally explained. However, the exact procedures of surveying and construction of these massive structures are not known to us because of the absence of contemporary written records.

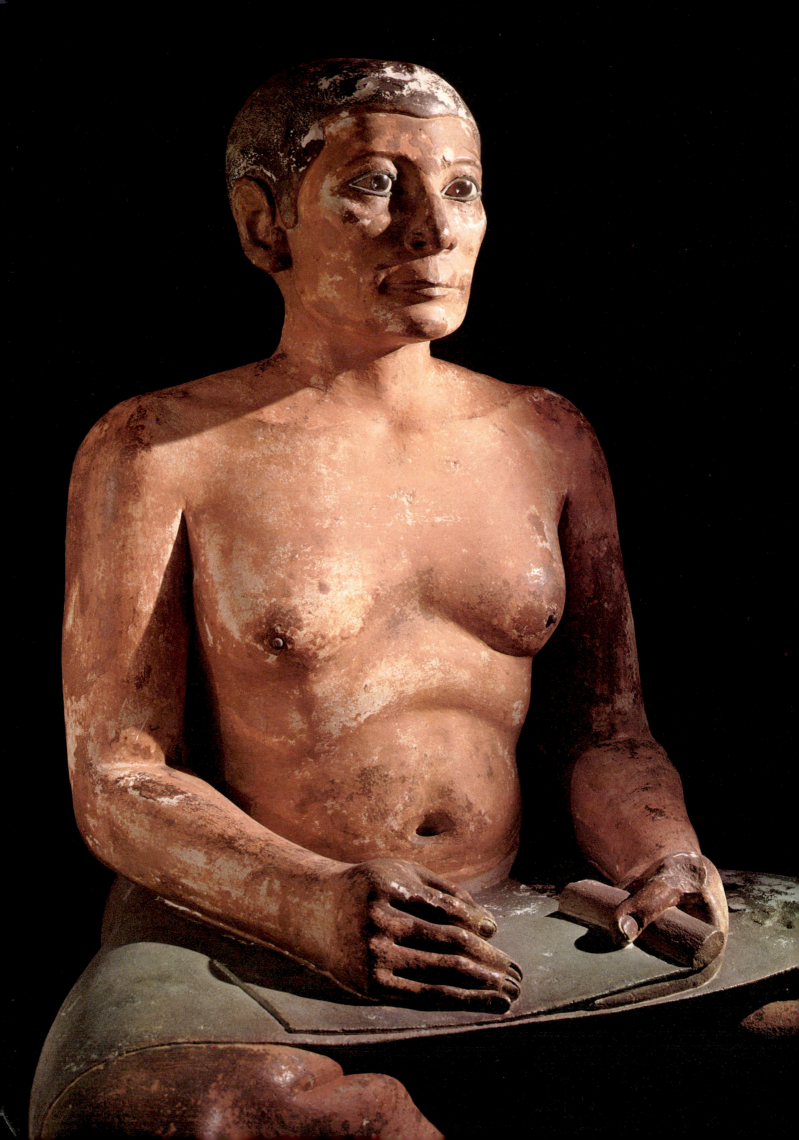

An important type of sculpture which remained unique to private statues was the representation of the tomb-owner as a scribe. Literacy was an essential qualification for a successful bureaucratic career, and the scribe-statues which were introduced towards the end of the Fourth Dynasty quickly became very popular. They show a man in the typical squatting posture of a scribe, reading or writing on a roll of papyrus spread on his lap. Most of these statues are very ordinary pieces, but the 'Scribe du Louvre', found in a late Fourth or early Fifth Dynasty tomb at Saqqara, and known by its present location, is probably the best private sculpture made during the Old Kingdom.

Right: Although the technique of relief uses the same conventions, and a similar approach to portraying reality, as painting on a flat surface, it is three-dimensional and thus sensitive to a play of light. The third dimension of Egyptian relief of the Old Kingdom, its height or depth, amounted to no more than a few millimetres. Depending on whether the represented feature is above or below the surrounding plain, the relief is 'raised' or 'sunk'. When the surface was exposed to direct sunlight, sunk relief was preferred because it relies on the strong contrast between light and shadow. Raised relief was chosen for decoration illuminated by diffused light. The alabaster panel of Rawer of the mid-Fifth Dynasty, decorated in sunk relief, was found at the back of a niche in his tomb at Giza.

It included only the groups of rulers regarded by its compiler as the most illustrious and worthy of commemoration, while the kings of the less famous periods of Egyptian history were simply omitted. At its beginning it presents a series of fifty-six names, introduced by that of Meni (Menes of Manetho), and is the most complete record of successive kings of the earliest part of Egyptian history.

To the eyes of an outsider the initial impression of ancient Egypt is one of unfamiliarity. The astonishment of the stranger encountering Egyptian civilization for the first time is nothing new. No one has conveyed it better than Herodotus who visited Egypt in the second half of the fifth century BC. 'In Egypt the women go to market and sell the produce, while the men remain at home weaving; and their weaving technique involves pushing down the weft, which in other countries is pushed upwards. Egyptian men carry loads on their heads, the women on their shoulders. The women urinate in a standing position, the men sitting down. . . . Elsewhere priests grow their hair long: in Egypt they shave themselves. The common custom of mankind in mourning is for the bereaved to cut their hair short: Egyptians in the event of bereavement let both their hair and beards (which they normally shave) grow long. . . . For writing and for counting with pebbles the Greeks move their hands from left to right, the Egyptians from right to left. And despite this practice they claim that their own writing is "rightwards", while that of the Greeks is "leftwards".'

Although the development of ancient Egypt can be followed in detail through written records over the unparalleled span of some 3000 years and through archaeological artefacts for even longer, the unfamiliarity of the culture makes it difficult to see it as other than static and permanent. Egypt's ideological and political concepts seem to have been remarkably impervious to change. Egyptian art of all periods strikes us by the peculiarity of its forms of expression and apparent rigidity of conventions. The principles of the hieroglyphic system of writing endured little affected by the passing of time, from its emergence towards the end of the Pre-dynastic Period, around 3000 BC, to its last recorded instance in the temple at Philae near the first Nile cataract as late as AD 394.

Yet the first impressions are shown on closer examination to be mis-

Old Kingdom sources are strangely and surprisingly silent about the Giza sphinx. It was only some 1,000 years after the Sphinx had been made, during the Eighteenth Dynasty of the New Kingdom, that it was mentioned. At this period it was thought to represent the sky-god Haremakhet ('Horus on the Horizon') or the Syrian deity Hauron.

Right: The eastern part of the enclosure containing Netjerikhet's step pyramid was occupied by stone replicas of kiosks and chapels for the celebration of the royal jubilee-festivals (heb-sed). It is likely that during the Old Kingdom these festivals took place at Ineb-hedj (Memphis), the first after 30 years of the king's reign. Netjerikhet's heb-sed structures were provided for the jubilee the king hoped to enjoy in afterlife. Parts of the cult temples of the developed pyramid-complexes may have served a similar purpose, but Netjerikhet's arrangements remain unique. Some of the elements of the buildings which are currently being restored at Saqqara are modern.

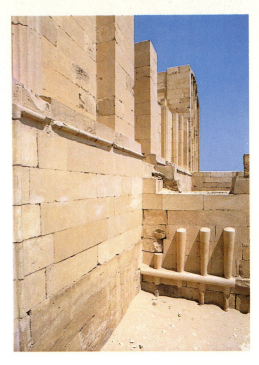

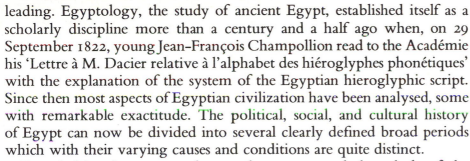

leading. Egyptology, the study of ancient Egypt, established itself as a scholarly discipline more than a century and a half ago when, on 29 September 1822, young Jean-François Champollion read to the Académie his 'Lettre à M. Dacier relative à l'alphabet des hiéroglyphes phonétiques' with the explanation of the system of the Egyptian hieroglyphic script. Since then most aspects of Egyptian civilization have been analysed, some with remarkable exactitude. The political, social, and cultural history of Egypt can now be divided into several clearly defined broad periods which with their varying causes and conditions are quite distinct.

Egypt's historic era started around 2925 BC, and the whole of the country had come under the authority of one ruler only a little earlier. The formative stage of the Egyptian state corresponds to the first two royal dynasties of Manetho and the first fourteen kings of the Abdju (Abydos) list, and was completed around 2658 BC. The Old Kingdom, which was thus ushered in without any perceptible break, produced and sustained the first flourishing of ancient Egyptian civilization in all its aspects. Egyptian society quickly achieved a high degree of economic prosperity as the result of the efficiency and organizational abilities of its officials, and a high cultural standard because of the skills and talents of its craftsmen and artists. It was a period of prosperity, stability, confidence, and self-assurance, an era during which the Egyptians first realized their ambitions and aspirations, and became the most advanced civilization of their time. Even the notoriously 'unhistorically'-minded Egyptians of later times used to look to the Old Kingdom for religious, cultural, and moral inspiration. For us, Old Kingdom pyramids and tombs, with their magnificent reliefs and paintings, statues and stelae, often epitomize the whole of ancient Egypt and the achievement of its civilization.

The Old Kingdom lasted for over 500 years (2658–2135 BC), and corresponds to the Third to Eighth Dynasties of Manetho. Its kings are represented by the fifteenth to fifty-sixth names of the Abdju list. The sharp decline at the end of the Old Kingdom and during the following period affected Egyptian society at all levels. When the collapse approached, the Egyptians themselves felt that their world was coming to an end. 'What had never happened has now happened' was how a sage called Neferti described it. 'The land turns round as does a potter's wheel' were the words of another prophet of doom, Ipuwer.

Above: Structures in wood and various perishable materials were faithfully and deliberately copied in stone in Netjerikhet's enclosure, but it would be wrong to assume that this was because stone architecture had at first to rely entirely on forms developed in other materials. Here it was a recognition of stone as the material in which to build for eternity, a concept which was to remain valid for the rest of Egyptian history.

Above left: While under construction, the design of Netjerikhet's traditionally conceived stone-built mastaba was modified five times, as if the architect was gradually becoming aware of the possibilities of the new building material and did not wish to miss the opportunity to capitalize on them as work progressed. It was changed as a result of an enlargement of its ground plan, but more importantly by a sudden adoption of a four-stepped, and later six-stepped, silhouette. Imhotep, the alleged architect in charge of the project, later became one of the few private persons deified in Egypt. His connection with Netjerikhet was confirmed by the discovery of the base of Netjerikhet's statue with Imhotep's name inscribed on it.

TWO

THE BEGINNINGS

In the vizier Mereruka's early Sixth Dynasty tomb at Saqqara, a papyrus thicket is dramatically depicted alive with animals and birds. The water is teeming with fish, and three baying hippopotami are harpooned by men in boats. Locusts resting on some rushes provide a haven of peace in the commotion which reigns all around them.

ANCIENT EGYPTIAN CIVILIZATION owed its existence to the unique combination of physical conditions found in the north-eastern corner of the African continent from *c.* 10,000 BC. About a half of the Black Land (*Kemet*), as it was called by its inhabitants, was little more than a narrow strip of an extremely fertile dark soil deposited by the nameless River (*iteru*) and annually replenished by the waters of the inundation. The stream flowed on its journey to the north through an extensive region of Nubian sandstone, but this in southern Egypt gave way to limestone beyond the present Esna. When it passed the Ineb-hedj district ('White Wall', later Mennufer or Memphis in Greek), it divided into a series of smaller branches which spread like the fingers of a hand before reaching the Mediterranean shore, thus creating the wide expanse of alluvial land known to us as the Nile Delta. It was a marshy area containing a large number of unstable river channels, and permanent habitation was only possible on the Delta's margins and on sporadically occurring sandy ridges ('turtle-backs') which remained out of reach of water even at the height of inundation. These watery regions were full of wildlife, and an almost obligatory scene in the Old Kingdom tomb-scene repertoire showed the tomb-owner spearing fish and hunting birds with a throw-stick from a small papyrus skiff in swamps.

The extent of marsh-land in the Nile valley itself was limited. A chain of oases to the west provided focal points for settlers, but otherwise only a poor and sparsely inhabited country stretched on either side of the Black Land. For much of the early history of ancient Egypt, until about 2350 BC, the deserts, particularly their borders and the tracts adjacent to the wadis, were not entirely arid and barren because of the generally moister climate with some periodic rainfall. These parts of the desert supported savanna-type vegetation with trees and shrubs, and were the habitat of a variety of wildlife. The most significant factor in the environmental changes which occurred in the Nile valley before the beginning of the Sixth Dynasty was man, whose farming activities deprived many of the animals and birds of their natural breeding grounds, and who purposefully tried to eliminate animals harmful to him or his crops.

Only reluctantly the Egyptians ventured outside the Nile valley. The hills in the desert to the east were rich in valued minerals and metals, in particular copper and gold. The same held true of Nubia, the land beyond the acknowledged southern frontier formed by the granite barrier of the first Nile cataract. In addition, Nubia also possessed the precious commodity of which Egypt was so painfully short—wood. In the north-east, the Sinai peninsula became the source of copper and the semi-precious

Forms of Predynastic pottery varied from simple bowls, cups, and tall vases to curious forms on feet, or pots consisting of two connected cylinders. Although usually made without the help of any mechanical device, the standard of Predynastic pottery was not surpassed in historic times.

stone turquoise, though both were perhaps at first imported rather than mined by the Egyptians. Goods from more distant countries reached Egypt by sea or overland through these desert regions, and the commercial routes had to be safeguarded. Military expeditions were sent out to deal ruthlessly with the occasional threat to the inhabitants of the Nile valley settlements posed by roving bands of the nomadic 'sand-dwellers' (*heryu-sha*) of the desert. On the whole, however, Egypt's safety in isolation within its natural geographical frontiers and its self-sufficiency in almost all respects were among the most important circumstances which influenced the formation of the character and attitudes of its inhabitants.

The annual inundation is caused by the summer monsoon rains outside Egypt, in the mountains of Ethiopia and the southern Sudan, though the

reason for it was never understood by the Egyptians. Most of the land in the valley and the Delta which was naturally flooded when the Nile rose, remained under water for some ten weeks between August and November. The difference between the highest and the lowest level of the Nile was over eleven metres (thirty-five feet) in southern Egypt, some seven metres in the Ineb-hedj district, and about three metres in the Delta. When the river left its natural bed, the heavier of the materials carried by its flood-waters were deposited first so that levees gradually formed close to the Nile banks in the valley and separated the main stream from the low-lying basins beyond. Water stayed in these seasonally flooded basins long after the inundation ended, and each year a fresh deposit of sediment rich in organic matter was left behind.

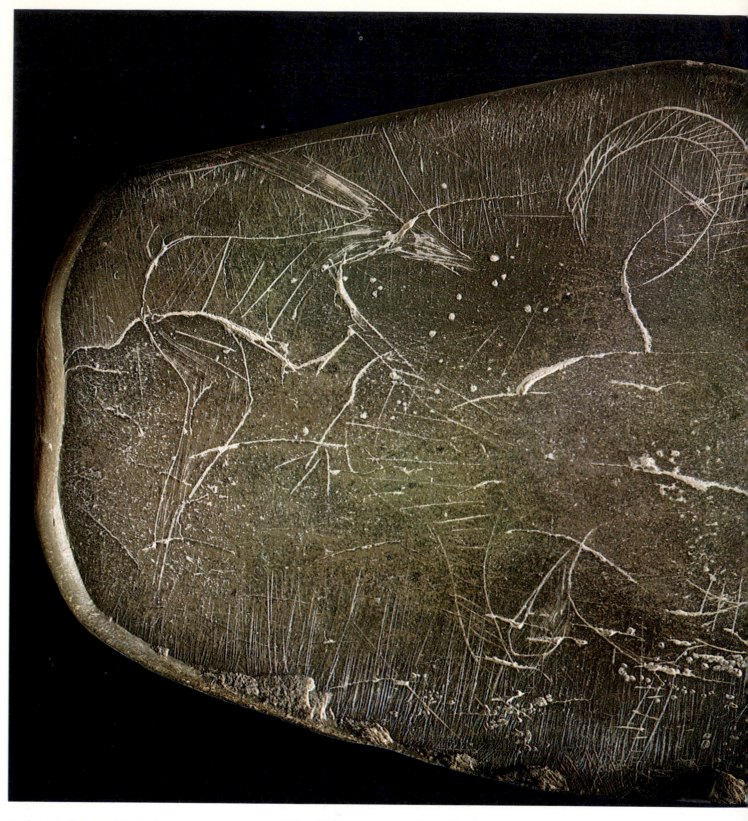

Predynastic (Nagada I Period) cosmetic palette with finely incised representations of desert animals. The drawings are in subject, style, and execution strongly reminiscent of the early rock art of the Eastern Desert and Nubia.

The Nile is very predictable, but the relationship between man and the river was so delicately balanced and his dependence on it so complete that an occasional deviation from its usual timetable and its normal volume of water had very serious consequences. Surprisingly, the Egyptians had no deity of the River as such, but the fertile aspects of inundation, *hapy*, were portrayed in the form of a grotesquely fat man with a huge paunch and pendant breasts, the image of well-being and prosperity.

There is little evidence that any of the changes which took place along the Nile before the beginning of the historic era were due to migrations of

population from outside Egypt. On the contrary, it appears that basically the same, even if not homogeneous, physical types persisted throughout all of the prehistoric and historic periods. The environmental conditions in Shemau (the southern valley, or Upper Egypt) and Ta-mehu (the northern Delta, or Lower Egypt), were in sharp contrast. The geographical shape of the country was unique—nearly 900 km (600 miles) long, but in the valley only exceptionally as much as twenty km (twelve miles) wide. Along this frontier there would have been contacts with different peoples sufficient to produce variations attested in skeletal

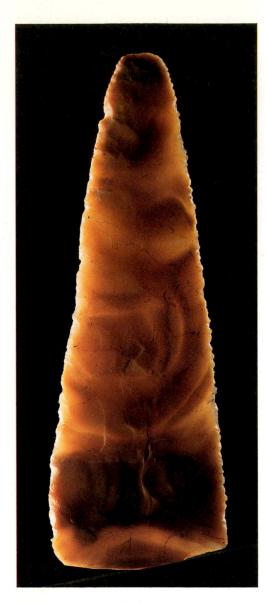

remains. The inhabitants of Upper Egypt were on the whole of a smaller, gracile type with long narrow skulls, compared with the taller and more heavily built mesocephalic Lower Egyptians. On monuments, all men have dark curly hair and their bodies are dark red to indicate the heavily sunburnt light-brown skin (brown was absent from the palette of the Egyptian artist). The conventional depiction of the lighter complexion of women was yellow.

A similar picture of population stability is obtained from an analysis of the Egyptian language, even though the variety of current opinions is as great as in the case of physical anthropology. Connections exist with ancient and modern Semitic languages of western Asia, as well as Cushitic, Berber and Chado-Hamitic languages of Ethiopia, Libya and the western Sudan. These, however, suggest a common origin rather than a super-imposition of one language upon another. The prehistoric inhabitants of Egypt and the historic Egyptians therefore spoke the same language in different stages of its development. It was only after proper texts (rather than names, titles, lists, or short descriptions accompanying representations) appeared during the Fourth Dynasty that we can study it in detail, but some of the features of the earlier phase of spoken Egyptian were preserved in the religious literature of the Old Kingdom.

The time between the Palaeolithic (Stone Age) civilization and the rise of the first Egyptian dynasty of kings is conveniently described as the Predynastic (Neolithic) Period. The most significant advance made at that time was the introduction of settled agriculture. Each year when the inundation receded, conditions in the Nile valley were suitable for primitive farming. The water which was left in naturally created flood-basins could with little effort be made to last for most of the growing season of any seed which may have been sown. The pattern of farming in the Predynastic Period varied from one place to another in order to exploit local conditions to the maximum, but for much of the early history of Egypt there was little need for large-scale artificial irrigation of the fields under cultivation and the matter was left in the hands of local communities. Even during the Old Kingdom the role of the

Above, this page and facing page :
Implements made of flint were gradually increasing in number and quality to attain their peak before the end of the Predynastic Period, although copper was already used for the same purpose. In flint-making, high skills, and therefore specialization, were needed for mining the raw material and for the masterly craftsmanship displayed in some of the pieces found at late Predynastic and early Dynastic sites.

state in maintaining the irrigation system remained distinctly limited.

The agricultural techniques and implements required for this early form of cereal cultivation were simple, and the change to settled farming was probably made easier by previous experimentation involving wild grains. Among finds of the Predynastic cultures are flint blades with serrated edges which were inserted in wooden sickle-handles used for reaping, circular threshing floors, granaries lined with wickerwork for storing the grain, and simple stone querns, or hand-mills, for grinding it. Emmer wheat and barley were the cereals cultivated, and although Asia is usually thought to have been their origin, Ethiopia is also a possibility.

The regular occurrence of favourable conditions for agriculture encouraged the establishment of settlements, often on the levees, which stayed dry during the inundation, and on the margins of the floodplain. The earliest villages perhaps were only semi-permanent, with primitive huts constructed of poles, reeds, and mats, but towards the end of the Predynastic Period there were fortified 'towns' with brick-built rectangular houses consisting of a roofed room and an open forecourt. Nubt (modern Nagada) and Nekhen (Hierakonpolis, modern Kom el-Ahmar) were the two Upper Egyptian towns in the forefront of this development. The view that the settling of the Nile region resulted from rapidly growing desiccation is unfounded. The climatic conditions remained relatively stable during the Predynastic Period and those changes in food production which occurred were due to the early settlers' grasp and exploitation of the favourable circumstances along the Nile. The population growth resulted both from the rising birth-rate and the increasing number of people settling in the region on a permanent basis.

Cattle, goats, sheep, pigs, and donkeys were the domestic animals, as well as dogs, but at this early period there were as yet no cats. Most of these animals probably reached Egypt from Asia via Sinai, but the local contribution to their domestication seems to have been small. Hunting and fishing continued to play a significant, if gradually diminishing, part in the economy, and arrow-heads, throw-sticks, and fish-hooks are frequently found in excavations.

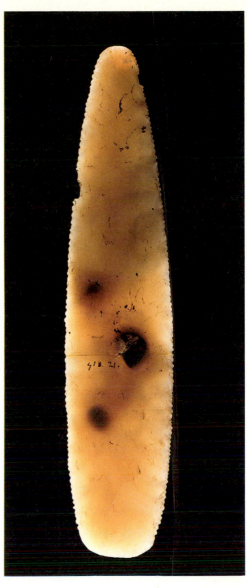

Flat cosmetic palettes ranged from simple rectangular shapes to elegant forms which imitated animals such as hippopotami, elephants, antelope, sheep, turtles, fish, and birds.

The most impressive element of some of the palettes is design in harmony with form. These patterns and solutions of spatial problems were imitated for the rest of Egyptian history. The 'Two Dogs Palette' was found at Nekhen (Hierakonpolis). Because of the haphazard distribution of the animals on the reverse of the palette, it is usually regarded as earlier than other pieces with a more orderly arrangement closer to the registers of Dynastic art. Such an explanation, however, may underestimate the sophistication of the design. For the Egyptians, the deserts bordering on the Nile valley were the home of wild animals and mythical beasts, and represented chaos. Within the symmetrically carved leaping dogs, the creatures of the desert present a mêlée of forms, postures, and movements, the very picture of disorder. Two long-necked animals are shown on the obverse.

The earliest sites with Predynastic remains date from about 5000–4500 BC. From then on, the development of prehistoric civilization can be followed continuously until the beginning of the First Dynasty, but not everywhere and not in full at all archaeological sites so far located. The chances of preservation and the changes which have taken place in the appearance of the valley and the Delta since then account for the patchy pattern. The successive stages of this development, or archaeological cultures, are known by the names of the villages near which their cemeteries or settlements were first recognized, or where they are particularly well attested. The Predynastic Period of northern Egypt is poorly known, but much of the country soon displayed considerable cultural unity. Nagada was the main culture from about 4000 BC, though at first confined to the south. It is usually divided into phase I (formerly called Amratian, after the site of Amra) and the later phase II (formerly Gerzean, after Gerza), which immediately preceded the rise of the First Dynasty.

In the absence of written records we have to rely entirely on artefacts for our knowledge of Predynastic society and its level of material culture.

Whether metallurgy evolved in Egypt independently or whether it was introduced from Palestine is a matter of some dispute. In southern Egypt, copper was known from the very beginning of the Predynastic Period, but initially it was very scarce and only used for the manufacture of small decorative items such as beads, and was thus regarded as a precious rather than a useful material. During Nagada II it became sufficiently common for its uses to be extended, and the opportunity was eagerly seized, as attested by the finds of copper axes, adzes, knives, daggers, awls, pins, and needles. Other metals, such as gold, silver, and even meteoric iron, were mostly used for the making of personal ornaments. Metal-working was one of the earliest industries which required specialization and separated craftsmen from the vast majority of farmers.

Stone was used for the manufacture of implements as well as weapons, among which the disc-shaped and later pear-shaped maceheads were the most prominent. The production of stone vessels reached a remarkably high standard towards the end of the Predynastic Period when they were made in large quantities. A variety of materials were employed, some very hard, including porphyry, basalt, schist, alabaster, and limestone. Cosmetic palettes used for grinding malachite (copper ore), and to a lesser degree galena (lead ore), for preparation of the popular green or black eye-paint, were also made of stone, in particular green schist. In the Predynastic Period the knowledge of small-scale stone-working was wide-ranging. It provided a starting point for the development which culminated in the tremendously rapid advances when monumental architecture in stone appeared at the beginning of the Third Dynasty.

In pottery, coarse utilitarian 'kitchen' ware, as well as very fine vessels with incised, painted, or other decoration, is known from the Predynastic Period. Some of the decorated pots were specially made to be deposited in graves and can be seen as the earliest evidence for workshops specializing in the manufacture of objects for the necropolis. Flax was grown, and weaving is attested by finds of spindle whorls and surviving examples of coarse linen, but skins and leather were also used for making clothes.

The time preceding the first Egyptian dynasties may be characterized as a period of modest beginnings, but very able experimentation in Egyptian art. The variety of forms of artistic expression is surprising, and it was lack of opportunities and incentives to create on a larger scale rather than a lack of ability which restricted the artist.

At this early period the term 'art' has to encompass personal ornaments and applied art, i.e. decorated objects of everyday life. Religious and

aesthetic feelings went hand in hand from the very beginning of Egyptian civilization and cannot always be easily separated. Apart from the simple design and decoration of their 'kitchen' pottery, the personal feelings and preferences of ordinary Egyptians are revealed in the decorative items they wore on their bodies or clothes. These were very often made up of beads of various materials and can be reconstructed to form necklaces and belts or girdles. Shells were used for the same purpose. Bracelets and armlets of shell, bone, or ivory were worn, as well as rings, pendants, and small amulets, some of them representing animals, birds, or fish.

The obverse of the so-called Battlefield Palette shows standards of deities, represented by a hawk and an ibis which, provided with human arms, are escorting bound captives. Such a curious addition of human elements was already very characteristic of the late Predynastic Period, and similar artistic devices were common in later times. The bordered circular depression on the right is all that still reminds us that the original purpose of such objects was for grinding eye-paint.

Below: Elaborate hairdos must have been fashionable because ornamental haircombs and long pins, usually made of ivory and often crowned with a beautifully observed figure of an animal or bird, were common.

The other side of the palette-fragment shown opposite. A guinea-fowl (?) is represented above a long-necked animal, perhaps a gazelle rather than a giraffe. The animal is one of two which originally flanked a date-palm in a symmetrical fashion. This is probably one of the motifs which Egyptian art adopted from abroad at the end of the Predynastic Period.

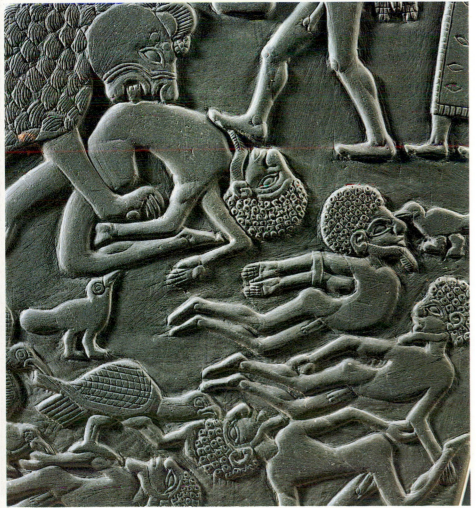

A number of votive palettes and mace-heads show very sensitive modelling, such as can be seen here in a detail of the obverse of the same Battlefield palette. It shows a lion and vultures preying on bodies after a battle. The provenance of the object is not recorded, but the area of Abydos seems very probable. It is difficult to date items of this type. Nevertheless, it appears that one or two generations may have been sufficient for the new artistic concepts to be realized, as if pent-up potential had suddenly been given a means of expression; this is the feeling gained from observation of many other features of late Predynastic art.

Ornamental palettes used for the preparation of make-up, decorated containers, spoons, and ladles of bone or ivory also belong to the category of toilet articles.

Some of the artistic effort was directed towards grave goods and indicates developed ideas concerning life after death. Many of the pots from Nagada II graves are painted in red on a buff background with representations of people, animals, and in particular large boats propelled by many oarsmen. The boats may carry shrines with standards of local gods attached to them, but it is equally possible that we have here a reflection of the rudimentary ideas concerning funerary boat-voyages known from the Old Kingdom. A unique multicoloured tomb-painting on plaster was found in the so-called Decorated Tomb at Nekhen (Hierakonpolis). It was probably made for one of the local Predynastic chiefs, and its scenes show boats, with human figures and animals engaged in a variety of activities. The representations of people are primitive in their execution and similar to those known from rock-drawings in Wadi Hammamat and Nubia, and the spatial distribution of elements is as haphazard as on the pottery. Few features, such as the half-hearted attempt to place one group on a common base-line, can be even remotely connected with the conventions of Egyptian dynastic art.

Small statuettes of animals, such as lions, hippopotami, jackals, and hawks, and of people, made of clay, ivory, or stone, are occasionally found in Predynastic graves. They show a remarkably high degree of stylization and abstraction. A limited number of objects were made for the presumed primitive shrines or 'temples' intended for the worship of gods. One large structure which is interpreted in this way is an oval stone-built enclosure filled with clean sand at Nekhen (Hierakonpolis). It is similar in shape to the hieroglyph with which the name of the place was written. Even if its dating to the late Predynastic Period is correct, it represents a special local form of sanctuary which was not comparable to those existing elsewhere and could not have influenced their development.

The most accomplished specimens of art are votive palettes, mace-heads, and knife-handles, decorated in relief. These objects were made for the highest echelon of late Predynastic society as Egypt began to enter its historic age. The decorated slate palettes and limestone mace-heads had lost their original practical purpose, and now became a convenient medium for expressing some of the tenets of nascent state ideology. This early Egyptian 'court' art seems to have been concerned more with the king than the god for whose temple the votive object was intended, as if the ruler wanted to placate and impress the deity by his own status and thus tried to ensure for himself a continued success. This, rather than an attempt to record real historical events, probably inspired such early works of art.

Some of the motifs (a man dominating a pair of lions, long-necked animals, interlacing serpents, rosettes, a griffin) and details (headdresses and robes) can be sought in Mesopotamia, but this does not mean that the objects were made outside Egypt or that the artists were brought from abroad. At a time when the Egyptians were moulding their own style it would have been natural that their top artists, who were working for a very exclusive clientele, were more susceptible to outside artistic inspiration and more prone to experimentation than in later times when a tradition and style set in. Trade contacts would have been sufficient to account for this. With a few exceptions, these influences from outside Egypt can be detected only in the official art of the late Predynastic Period, and betray a substantial gap which had quickly developed between the very small ruling élite and the rest of the population. It was this 'court' art,

Opposite: The makers of early Predynastic statues knew as yet none of the conventions of later Egyptian three-dimensional art, which results in the curiously un-Egyptian impression their creations exert. This statuette, made of the hard basalt, is known as the 'MacGregor Man', after the Rev. William MacGregor in whose collection it was until 1922.

Below: Three colossi of the ithyphallic god Min were found at Gebtiu (Koptos, modern Qift). These statues, originally four metres (thirteen feet) tall, but now badly battered, are the only known examples of monumental temple sculpture of the late Predynastic Period, even though their dating is not as secure as one would wish. This way of portraying the god Min was to last for the rest of Egyptian history.

25

produced by professional artists/craftsmen, which eventually led to the creation of the characteristic Egyptian style, while the art of the people was left behind and ceased at this point to exert any further influence.

Several inventions are thought to have been introduced to Egypt from abroad (Palestine, Syria and Mesopotamia) during the late Predynastic Period, such as the cylinder seal, certain forms of pottery, and brick niche architecture ('palace façade'). Long-distance trade is well documented by finds of imported materials (obsidian, lapis lazuli, turquoise, copper, possibly silver, ivory, Red Sea shells, wood, etc.), but the routes along which these items arrived in Egypt at this time can only be guessed.

During the Predynastic Period the Egyptians successfully learnt to exploit conditions along the Nile and developed an economic system based on mixed farming which was capable of satisfying the basic material needs of everyone settled in the region. The society whose picture emerges from the disjointed pieces of information available to us was based on village communities. Communal granaries found at some sites suggest a certain degree of very early organization at a local level. The need to control the division of the land for agriculture each year after the flood, and the advantages which accrued from a joint planning and maintenance of local dikes and canals, led to the emergence of chiefs who exerted authority over limited areas.

In the absence of outside interference the stimuli for further changes and the eventual creation of the unified Egyptian state had to come from within existing society. Inner pressures for development became apparent towards the end of the Predynastic Period. Growing craft specialization significantly enlarged the small section of people who did not directly take part in food production, and helped to deepen the incipient social stratification of Egyptian society. In the Nagada II period the differences in the social status were clearly reflected in the types and sizes of graves and the quality of burial goods. The demands and expectations of the privileged group of local chiefs could only be satisfied through more advanced ways of social organization. At the same time, regional characteristics, such as more favourable farming conditions, proximity to mineral resources, or control of long-distance trade routes, created differences among local communities. These strains and contradictions led to conflict and the formation of larger political units towards the end of the Predynastic Period. The ease of communication by the river must have helped this development. The trend reached its logical conclusion when all desirable land along the Nile had been incorporated within the limits of control by one ruler. Although the precise steps of this process are not known to us, there is little doubt that it took place over a period of time and was one of gradual expansion and annexation rather than large-scale confrontation. The formation of an Egypt united in a political sense was accomplished at the latest around 2950 BC under King Narmer, and this situation was to last until the end of the Old Kingdom, more than 800 years later.

The sequence of events which led to the appearance of the Egyptian state towards the end of the Predynastic Period is often described as unification. The term must not be interpreted as conveying the idea of a struggle between two political entities which ended in the victory of the South (Upper Egypt) and the subjugation of the North (Lower Egypt). As on several occasions in later history, the initiative did, indeed, come from the South, where the stimuli for a change were always stronger. There is, however, no clear evidence for a showdown between two large kingdoms. The significance of the scenes on the decorated palettes and mace-heads is by no means certain, and although the distinction between

Predynastic statuettes strike us by their unusual portrayal of the human figure. Woman is often shown with a summarily indicated head, prominent breasts, a slender waist, and heavy hips. Sculptures of this type in ivory have no arms, but those made of clay show arms reminiscent of the wings of a bird raised above the head (hence the term 'bird deity'), as if supporting a vessel the woman may have carried on her head. The material from which the statuette was made no doubt caused the difference in style. Man, on the other hand, is usually represented as a squat rectangular block with a triangular bearded head and large eyes.

Upper and Lower Egypt was stressed from very early times, this may have been a convenient administrative division—and one reflecting obvious physical reality—when the capital was established not far from the apex of the Delta at the beginning of the First Dynasty. One of the peculiarities of Egyptian thinking was the notion of dualism, i.e. a totality consisting of two elements in harmonious opposition. The concept was founded in Egyptian geography as well as early history. The country lends itself to such an approach easily: the known world = The Black Land (*Kemet*) + The Red Land (*Deshret*, the desert); Egypt = the valley (Upper Egypt) + the Delta (Lower Egypt). Historically, the earliest towns in Upper Egypt, where the idea would have developed, were Nekhen and Nubt, the homes of the rival gods Horus and Seth. Already Predynastic rulers wore two insignia on their heads, the White Crown and the Red Crown, and the royal title which was introduced in the reign of King Den of the First Dynasty and which was closest to our 'king' was *ni-sut-bit*, literally 'One who belongs to the Sedge (= Upper Egypt) and the Bee (= Lower Egypt).' This way of thinking must have appeared long before it found its reflection in iconography or texts, and to regard the occurrence of twin elements, such as the royal crowns, as evidence for the existence of two independent kingdoms in late Predynastic Egypt, amounts to looking at things through our own eyes, rather than seeing them the way the Egyptians did.

Interpretation of the very limited inscriptional evidence from the end of the Predynastic Period is difficult because of the primitive state of writing at the time, and it is unlikely that more informative sources will ever be found. Attempts to demarcate the stages leading to the creation of one Egyptian state from the geographical distribution of pottery bearing royal names hardly represents an infallible method. Trade invariably precedes conquest, and the pots with their contents could have been acquired by peaceful means. Political events are notoriously difficult to trace in ordinary archaeological material, and Predynastic Egypt is no exception to the rule.

Some areas were to be only gradually incorporated into Egypt. The region south of Nekhen may not have been annexed before the end of the Second Dynasty, and much of the north-eastern Delta did not form part of the Egyptian provincial system even during the Old Kingdom, probably because it was not thought to be economically viable. The political unification achieved in the late Predynastic Period thus did not represent the end, but only the most important phase, of a continuous dynamic process of establishing the natural frontiers of Egypt.

Manetho had at his disposal records of kings going back to King Menes, but this name may be completely fictitious and based on a word-play which was misunderstood as a royal name by the later compilers of king-lists. The first historic king in the Manethonian definition was Athothis, or Teti as he appears in the Abdju (Abydos) list, the second king of Manetho's First Dynasty. It was during his reign, in about 2925 BC, that the first year-lists ('annals') appeared, and that provided the earliest point of Egyptian history which Manetho, some 2650 years later, could trace. Hence it became the beginning of his history of Egypt. The traditional beginning of Egypt's First Dynasty and its historic era was thus fixed by the introduction of an administrative practice and perhaps compounded further by a misunderstanding, and had little direct connection with the appearance of the first Egyptian king, the creation of the Egyptian state, or the invention of script.

The more advanced of the votive palettes and ceremonial mace-heads of the late Predynastic Period already show a number of features usually associated with later reliefs: base-lines and rudimentary division of scenes into registers, intentional disregard for realistic relative sizes, and the typically Egyptian way of portraying the human figure. The two signs written next to the face of the king have been interpreted as his title and name, hence the term King 'Scorpion'. Such an interpretation, however, is almost certainly wrong. The scorpion is a large ceremonial image, as shown by the vertical projection probably representing a tang for insertion into a pole or mast, and does not record the king's name. If King 'Scorpion' is thus refuted, the likeliest candidate for identification with the figure on the mace-head is Narmer.

THREE

GATHERING PACE

The excellent quality of animal sculpture is one of the least known aspects of Egyptian art. The representational and other conventions imposed on the artist were less rigid when portraying animals, and so he was able to create more freely. The statue of a seated lion from Nekhen (Hierakonpolis) is a masterly combination of observation of live animals and of highly stylized features and motifs. The connection with the king is indicated by the bib-like mane falling on the chest of the animal, reminiscent of the lappets of the royal headcloth. Although the statue is made of pottery—an unusual material for this type of sculpture—the artist succeeded in conveying the vigour and ferocity of the beast. The piece probably dates from the Third Dynasty, but it may be earlier.

THE EGYPTIANS VERY EARLY EVOLVED A calendar based on a year of 365 days. When this happened, and the precise way in which it was arrived at is not known, but observation of several astronomical phenomena or the rising of the Nile over a period of time would have been sufficient for its calculation. For reasons which may have been closely connected with the provisioning of officials and the rudimentary system of collecting taxes, the new state bureaucracy soon felt the need for a dating system which distinguished between different years so that they could be recorded. The numbering of years starting from a fixed point was not known, and so each year was described, or named, by one or more of its outstanding events. This method required a centrally-kept list of such eponymous happenings in order that dates could be checked and computed; these year-lists ('annals') were started during the reign of King Aha (Manetho's Athothis, and Teti of other lists). More often than not the chosen occasions were of religious significance rather than of general interest, and the 'annals' cannot be regarded as an attempt to record history in the sense of later chronicles.

The creation of the unified Egyptian state introduced a new ideological framework and a new political organization of the country, but changed little in the material situation of the majority of the Egyptian farming population, and left the basic methods of agricultural production unaffected. Few of the cultural advances made at this time had a direct bearing on the lives of ordinary peasants. Centralized government brought a degree of safety and political stability, and its greater resources provided better security against the consequences of natural disasters such as famine, but the greatest effect of the change was in the sphere of manufacturing. Changes in society increased a demand for certain types of goods. The largest customer was the state itself, personified by the king and his immediate family, and many items of everyday life were now also made for the growing numbers of officials. Craftsmen and artists had easier access to raw materials, and were able to specialize as a result of the larger market for their products. When need arose, the state could mobilize a manpower which, in both number and quality, had been undreamt of by local chiefs of the Predynastic Period.

Arts and industries, inasmuch as the distinction between them was in Egypt always rather tenuous, now came to the fore. Metal-working and crafts which benefited from the use of metal implements made tremendous progress. The two main metals in which the Egyptians worked were copper and gold, but the latter was restricted to decorative items. Copper tools and weapons with their edges hardened by hammering were now in

A gaming disc in black steatite, one of 45 made of various materials and variously decorated, found in the Saqqara mastaba of Hemaka, an official of King Den. The scene is in relief, and shows dogs chasing and despatching gazelles. The bodies of three of the animals are inlaid with alabaster.

common use by craftsmen, and vessels beaten out of sheets of metal were the chief innovation of the early dynasties. There was a variety of forms, including ewers, basins, and bowls, with their spouts and loop handles attached by rivets or wire.

Carpenters and cabinet-makers, working with native as well as imported woods, soon learnt all the essential techniques of joining. In addition to such prosaic items as doors, they manufactured household furniture, including beds, various chairs, stools, and chests, often decorated by fine carving or inlaid with ivory or faience. Leather upholstery of furniture was not uncommon, and the legs of chairs regularly terminated in ivory imitations of bull's hooves. Gameboards, some with pieces in the form of couchant lions, were very popular.

Jewellers used various materials, such as gold, copper, faience, shell, and ivory, together with a host of semi-precious stones, to make necklaces, bracelets, pendants, and amulets. Few of the more opulent examples are extant, but a remarkable discovery was made in the otherwise thoroughly plundered tomb of King Djer at Abdju (Abydos). A human arm swathed in linen in a primitive form of mummification, probably overlooked by robbers, was found with four bracelets still in place. One of the bracelets was made up of alternating gold and turquoise plaques shaped like a palace façade (*serekh*) with a hawk perched on top, symbolizing one of the royal names. The beads of various types in another bracelet included some made of amethyst and lapis lazuli.

Stone vessels of this period are the best from ancient Egypt, and are remarkable for their imaginative forms, often never to be repeated. Their makers were fond of imitating other materials, such as basketry, and although occasionally it may have been a simple adoption of a well-known motif, at other times it seems to have reflected a pure joy and exuberance in mastering the material and indulgence in showing off the creator's skill. A hand-held drill with a flint blade was the main tool of the trade, supplemented by a tubular drill and copper chisels. The flint industry continued to supply large quantities of blades for tools, particularly for everyday use by the poorer members of society.

Many specialized forms of mass-produced pottery were made, largely undecorated. Some were used for cooking, eating, and drinking, others

erved for storage of solid foodstuffs, such as fruit, cheese, meat, and even read, or as containers for liquids, including wine, beer, and milk, and yet thers as moulds for baking bread and cakes. Grain was stored in large ars.

While crafts and applied arts thrived as never before, monumental culpture, in the round and in relief, got off to a slow start. Only fragments f larger private statues in wood and of smaller pieces in stone have survived. The only known examples of royal sculpture in stone are two tatues of King Khasekhem at the end of the Second Dynasty. Statues of nimals, mostly lions and baboons, show features of abstraction and tylization in continuation of the Predynastic tradition. Much of these haracteristics disappeared in the developed, more naturalistic, art of the Old Kingdom. Small sculpture in stone, ivory, and faience was common, nd it is in these small figurines that we can follow the development from he Predynastic to the typical dynastic three-dimensional art.

Decorated palettes and mace-heads went out of fashion in the First Dynasty, together with any features which could be regarded as un-Egyptian. The art of relief-carving survived mainly in tomb-stelae gravestones), but Egyptian monumental relief could only develop ignificantly when the changes in state ideology and religion, and the rowing familiarity with the use of stone, found their expression in nonumental building. As yet the opportunities offered were few, and ntil the situation changed in the Third and Fourth Dynasties, the ability lisplayed at the end of the Predynastic Period could not manifest itself nore fully.

Our knowledge of official civil architecture, such as palaces, is almost ntirely second-hand, based on their representations or presumed similaries in tomb architecture. The same is true of early temples, but we are vell informed about tombs. Graves of ordinary people of the earliest eriod of Egyptian history were not richer or larger than their Predynastic ounterparts, but tombs built during the First Dynasty for kings, close nembers of the royal family, and the highest officials of the state, now ncreased enormously in size. The area of their superstructure was regurly in excess of a thousand square metres (10,000 square feet), and lthough working with unbaked mud-brick, Egyptian architects and

33

The stela of King Djet, from his tomb at Abdju (Abydos), illustrates the difficult step from relatively small objects to monumental relief. A number of royal stelae of the first two Dynasties are known, one or two of them of excellent craftsmanship, but they are inscribed solely with the name of the king and carry no scenes.

work supervisors were acquiring the knowledge and managerial skill needed in large-scale monumental building of the Old Kingdom. The burial chamber and some of the magazines for tomb provisions were soon dug in the gravel and rock substratum, and during the Second Dynasty became a veritable maze of underground corridors and rooms. Above ground, the tombs of the First Dynasty, particularly, presented a striking appearance with their whitewashed niche façades painted in lively multi-coloured patterns in imitation of wall-matting.

The stelae with the names of the owners, which were found connected with some of these tombs, were their only decorated stone elements. The material was, no doubt, chosen for its durability. The knowledge of working in stone and appreciation of its possibilities as a building material led to an occasional use of stone elements for flooring, roofing, or wall lining of rooms, and in the blocking of passages by portcullises. Not only limestone, but also the much harder granite from the southern Aswan region was employed.

At the beginning of the First Dynasty, a new administrative capital was founded and became known as Ineb-hedj, 'White Wall', presumably because of its appearance. A series of large tombs of high officials and some other members of the royal family were built in the desert cemeteries in this area, particularly at Saqqara. The site chosen for the capital was strategically located between the agriculturally important Delta with its contacts with western Asia, and the Nile valley with its access to gold and copper deposits and mineral resources, and was thus eminently suitable for administering both parts of the country. This caused some decline in the importance of the traditional centres in Upper Egypt, although they continued to enjoy religious prestige. The royal residence probably also moved to the north, but it is unlikely that the monarch remained at one place throughout the whole year. The kings of the First Dynasty, as well as Peribsen and Khasekhemui of the Second, were buried at Abdju (Abydos) next to several of their predecessors of the late Predynastic Period. The area and its local temple of the god Khentiamentiu (the 'Foremost of the Westerners', i.e. of the dead) may have already at that time been renowned as a religious centre, but this in itself would hardly have been a sufficient reason for the siting of royal tombs if there had not been other connections. It is likely that the Predynastic rulers whose successors eventually became kings of all Egypt originally came from this region. Royal tombs of the first half of the Second Dynasty probably were at Saqqara.

The king now enjoyed a unique status which elevated him above the rest of society. Ideologically, this must have represented a dramatic departure from the position held by the chiefs of the Predynastic Period. It is significant that no other figure which could be interpreted as being comparable to him appears on monuments before the beginning of the Old Kingdom. The concept of the king who is aloof, with only standards of deities accompanying and assisting him, emerged in Egyptian art at the time of unification. The king's duty was to govern the world and maintain its order.

The definition of the king's position in society had to reconcile his new royal status with some earlier concepts. One of these was the jubilee festival (*heb-sed*), the original purpose of which was probably a periodic renewal of the powers and vitality of the local chief. Now it became a ritual replay of the beginning of the reign.

The distinction between the group which gave Egypt its early élite, the ruling *paat*, and the rest of the populace, the *rekhyt*, was the main division in Egyptian society at the beginning of the historic era. The origins of uch social stratification, however, are not clear. It seems that at first all igh officials of state administration were royal relatives, particularly rinces, who to some extent shared the king's exalted position. The chasm vhich separated members of this élite from the rest of the population is raphically illustrated by the sizes of their tombs. Some of them, both oyal and those of high officials, were found surrounded by smaller graves vhich contained burials of retainers: members of the household and the arim, craftsmen, dwarfs and entertainers, and even dogs.

The picture of the earliest Egyptian administration is detailed, but ncomplete. Much of the evidence consists of official titles inscribed on essels and found on seal-impressions, and does not lend itself easily to nterpretation. The administrative system was, no doubt, diverse, and eed not be regarded as particularly complex, thorough, or all-embracing. t was centred on the palace and the person of the king, with royal relatives cting on the king's behalf in the provinces, but many of the characteristics f the earlier chiefdoms had survived. The 'annals' show that a census of ll Egypt took place every other year. It is likely that at first the king ravelled the country by river during the 'following of Horus' and super-ised the gathering of tribute. The 'treasurer of the king of Lower Egypt' sedjauty bity) was in charge of this primitive form of personally enforced ollection which eventually turned into more or less regular dispatches of roduce to the royal palace. This official became the most important gure in the administration. The heights of inundation on cultivated elds, so meticulously recorded in the 'annals', may have been used for ssessing the tax to be levied. Provisions for the palace and the royal tomb ame from royal estates in the Delta which were the responsibility of dj-mer officials recruited from royal princes.

The departments called the 'White House' (per-hedj) and the 'Red House' (per-desher) functioned as the state treasury. The received produce vas kept in specialized storehouses, and was used to pay officials, crafts-nen, and retainers, and was perhaps also distributed as donations to local emples and primitive funerary cult institutions. It also served as a means f exchange in foreign trade and in any other way the king deemed esirable. The distribution was in the hands of the 'master of the largess' hery wedjeb).

Village communities, although from the late Predynastic Period part of rger entities, continued to function as the smallest administrative units or the majority of the population. Theoretically, the political changes ffected them profoundly because the king now claimed sovereignty over ll land, in the same way as he was master over the fate of all people. In ractical terms, this did not at first manifest itself beyond the need to omply with occasional fiscal and other obligations imposed by the king hrough his provincial representatives. If it is possible to accept the basic otion of inequality which underlies it, and which the newly created tate now safeguarded, the political and economic system whose primitive orm appeared in Egypt at the beginning of the historic era was ideally natched to the conditions of the country and its society. It was to be the nost important factor in the further development during the Old ingdom.

We can conjecture that each of the larger chiefdoms at the end of the redynastic Period was connected with a cult-centre and a shrine or emple of the local deity. The fortunes of Egyptian gods waxed and vaned with those of their home districts, and the development of rela-onships among deities went side by side with the creation of one state. he king of the unified Egypt identified himself with the god Horus of Jekhen, but the appearance of Seth of Nagada as well as the god Horus in

The centrepiece on this ivory comb from Abydos is a serekh with the Horus-hawk (= the king) perching on top of it, and the name of King Djet written inside. Two was-sceptres symbolizing 'dominion', 'sovereignty', and an early form of the ankh-sign ('life') flank the serekh. Above, a bird's wings represent the sky, with a barque of an ancient form ferrying a hawk, perhaps the sun-god. Much of the symbolism in this group was employed by artists throughout the rest of Egyptian history.

the names of two kings of the late Second Dynasty need not be a reflection of civil strife, because the relationship between politics and religion cannot be reduced to a simple equation. Almost all of the deities of later times were known during the earliest dynasties, usually in the forms of animals, birds, or fetishes. The 'annals' often mention religious festivals and the foundation of establishments which probably represent temples, but we have very little information about them from elsewhere.

It is not clear to what extent donations of votive objects to temples and funerary cult institutions were accompanied by consumable goods. Evidence for an early form of economic organization attached to temples comes from stone vessels dating to the Second Dynasty. They were found at Saqqara, and inscribed on them is 'The King of Upper and Lower

Egypt, the Two Ladies, Ninetjer. The food-provisioning [*djefau*] of the goddess Bastet. The first priestly guild [*wer*]'. The source of this food for the goddess is not known.

Statues of gods were commonly made, according to the 'annals', but none of them has survived.

Beliefs concerning life after death were complex even at this early time. Tombs were regarded as houses of the dead, and royal, and even some private tombs, were on occasion accompanied by funerary palaces or model estates. This interpretation was strengthened during the Second Dynasty to the point where we can distinguish bedrooms, bathrooms, lavatories, and stalls for cattle in the tomb. A chapel against the north face of the superstructure of a Saqqara tomb dated to the reign of King Qaa probably served for funerary cult. Religious ideas of a different kind may be the reason for boat-burials near some tombs. Their purpose was to provide a means of transport for the celestial voyages which the deceased would undertake in afterlife. The gravel or sand mounds in the super-structure of other tombs may be connected with the concept of resurrection and the primeval mound on which life appeared.

Egypt's early contacts with the world outside the Nile valley fall into three categories: punitive military raids aimed at protecting and consolidating the frontiers, expeditions in order to bring various kinds of stone only occurring outside the valley, and long-distance trade. Most of the evidence for the supposed military expeditions against the inhabitants of the deserts comes from the 'annals'. 'Dates' of packaging or bottling on small labels which were attached to containers of foodstuffs provide other examples. 'The smiting of the Iuntyu-tribesmen' or 'the first occasion of the smiting of the East', are, unfortunately, rather vague indications, and may refer to ritual occasions rather than real events. The same may be true of representations of the king slaying an enemy which may be symbolic. However, there is evidence of an early military expedition to Nubia as far as the second cataract, which is recorded on a rock at Gebel Sheikh Suleiman near Wadi Halfa.

Conifer and cedar timber, now used in the construction of tombs and wherever quality wood was required, were obtained from coastal Syria and the Lebanon. Finds of large amounts of Syro-Palestinian pottery are interpreted as evidence for imports of olive oil and perhaps wine. The rest of the goods which were obtained by long-distance trade from Asia or Africa belonged to the luxury category, and included ebony, ivory, resins, obsidian, and lapis lazuli. Routes overland as well as by sea must have been used, and the western Delta seems to have played a particularly prominent role in the latter.

Some fourteen hundred years later, around 1250 BC, an anonymous scribe was copying the names of kings of the past on to an old sheet of papyrus for verification of documents in his office. When he came to the name of Djoser, he changed his reed pen and wrote the name in red, thus acknowledging the reputation Djoser (Netjerikhet) enjoyed at that time. It was not an attempt to mark the beginning of a completely new historic era. Manetho's Third Dynasty starts with Nekherophes, a Graecized form of the name of Nebka whose claim to fame otherwise is slight. To find the reasons for the change between Manetho's Second and Third Dynasties is not easy. Historians, ancient and modern, have tried to impose formal limits and dividing lines on the development of Egypt which started with the beginning of settled life in the Nile valley, but none of these markers are satisfactory. At best, they represent only milestones in the relentless, uninterrupted march towards the civilization usually described as the Old Kingdom.

Small ivory statuettes found in the temple at Nekhen (Hierakonpolis) may represent the beginnings of the typical 'dynastic' style in sculpture in the round, but their dating has not yet been established. Like this female dwarf with a massive wig, some of them probably belonged to items of furniture.

FOUR

ESTABLISHED AND BEAUTIFUL

'Pepy is Established and Beautiful.'★

The family group of Sonb is a fine example of vigorous composition rather than an outstanding work of art. The diminutive figure of the squatting dwarf, his seated wife, and two small children, have been successfully combined to form a pleasing group in which the dwarf's small stature, though not concealed, is made inconspicuous. Sonb held the titles of a 'servant of the god' (hem-netjer) of King Khufu and his successor Radjedef, and the statue was found in his tomb at Giza. This may suggest that he lived during the Fourth Dynasty, but a Sixth Dynasty date is more likely for this type of private sculpture.

IN THE PRESENCE OF THE SPECTACULAR ART and architecture of the Old Kingdom, with pyramids and tombs, one could easily forget that Egyptian society was for its existence entirely dependent on the production of its farmers. The simple agricultural tools and techniques known from representations in Old Kingdom tombs continued scarcely changed for the rest of the country's history. They were found sufficient for the tasks in hand and there was little inducement to improve them.

A selective panorama of farming life, accompanied by short conversations between farmworkers, was included in the repertoire of reliefs of many private tomb-chapels. Thus in one of them, of Sekhem-ankh-ptah of the middle of the Fifth Dynasty, the tomb-owner is described as 'watching the work in the fields: ploughing in the seed, reaping, pulling flax, loading donkeys, threshing with donkeys on threshing-floors, and winnowing'. These activities are shown in several registers before him, and were the main stages of the telescoped agricultural year as depicted by the sculptors who carved tomb-reliefs.

It is unlikely that the Egyptians of the Old Kingdom were able to obtain more than one crop annually. The year started with sowing when the inundation receded at the beginning of winter (ancient Egyptian *peret*, literally 'coming out' of either fields from under water, or seed), our October/November. The names of the most important cereals which were cultivated can be found on the so-called slab-stelae set up against the east face of the superstructures of some of the tombs built near the pyramid of King Khufu at Giza during the Fourth Dynasty. The tomb-owner is represented seated at a table before a long list of offerings, part of which consists of compartments in the form of small granaries with a description of their contents. On one of these stelae, of a 'scribe of divine books' whose name is lost, there are six such granaries with two varieties of barley (Hordeum hexastichon), Upper and Lower Egyptian (*it shema* and *it mehi*), emmer (Triticum dicoccum, *bedet*), an unidentified grain or fruit *besha*, wheat (Triticum aestivum, *sut*), and dates (*bener*), the last included because they were used in brewing beer.

Reliefs show that seed was scattered by hand from small baskets which the sowers carried over their shoulders, and was trodden in by a flock of sheep or a herd of goats, or was ploughed in with a yoke of oxen or cows. The ploughman was usually accompanied by another man urging on the animals. 'Go! ho, go!' shouts the drover of the oxen while encouraging

---

★ *The name of the pyramid of Pepy I at southern Saqqara.*

This page and facing page: Desert and river-bank scenes in the tomb of Ptahhotpe, of the late Fifth Dynasty, at Saqqara: hunting with dogs, cutting out the roes of fish, rope-manufacture, making papyrus rafts, netting fowl, and boatmen returning from the marshes engaged in a playful jousting tournament. These are just several miniature episodes from the large panorama of country life unfolding before two large figures of Ptahhotpe on the east wall of his offering-room (opposite two false-doors). To the uninitiated the size of the figures may seem unexpectedly small: the total height of the decorated area of the wall is some 5 Egyptian cubits (c.260 cm), and each of the seven horizontal registers is only between 29 and 43 cm high. The conscious striving to fill the available space entirely by representations and texts is particularly apparent in this tomb-chapel.

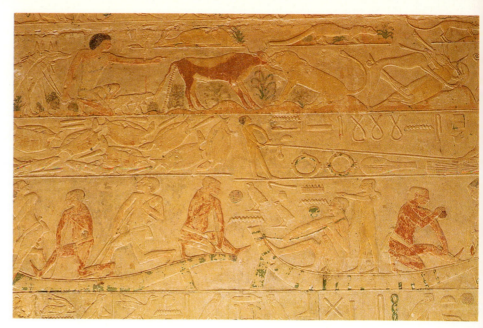

them not too gently with a stick, and 'under you, team!', probably reminding them to watch where they are treading. The most versatile of Egyptian agricultural tools, the hoe (*henen*), consisted of a wooden handle with a wooden 'blade' inserted in it by means of a tenon, and strengthened by a rope cross-tie. It was already in use in the Predynastic Period. A hieroglyph representing a plough (*heb*), made entirely of wood, first appeared in the Second Dynasty.

The corn ripened before the beginning of the Egyptian summer, between our February and April. Reaping was done with sickles of the same type as in the Predynastic Period. 'I am telling you, men, the barley is ripe, and he who reaps well will get it,' says the overseer to whom a sample sheaf is being shown for inspection in the tomb of Sekhem-ankh-ptah. 'What is it, then, men? Hurry up, our emmer is ripe!' the overseer goads the reapers in the Fifth Dynasty tomb of Ty at Saqqara. The cut corn was tied in sheaves which were put into large sacks ready for transport. 'Ho! donkey-herd of 2500!' is written in the Fifth Dynasty tomb of the vizier Akhtihotpe over the scene of animals brought in at top speed by men wielding sticks. The laden donkeys were led, some of them reluc-

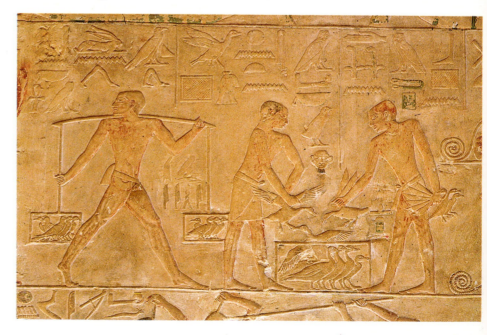

tantly, to improvised threshing-floors. 'Ho! go!' shouts one drover in the tomb of Sekhem-ankh-ptah, while a comrade advises him of a more effective method: 'Prod him in the rear, my friend!'

Flax-harvesting took place at about the same time, and representations of flax being pulled, tied into bundles, and transported on donkeys, often accompany the grain-harvest in Old Kingdom tombs.

Threshing was done by driving a herd of hoofed animals, usually cattle or donkeys, over sheaves of corn spread on a circular threshing-floor. The animals had to be kept on the move and not allowed to start helping themselves to grain, and the scene is usually one of seeming confusion, with men with sticks shouting at them and at each other at the top of their voices: 'Drive them round then!' 'Hey! I'll hit you if you turn round!' 'Watch what you are doing!'

Winnowing was done by sifting in hand-held sieves, or by tossing what was left on the threshing-floor, after the removal of straw, high in the air with wooden winnowing fans to allow a breeze to blow the chaff away. Unlike all the other agricultural tasks, this was carried out by women. 'Hurry up, my sister!' calls a farmhand at one of the women winnowing

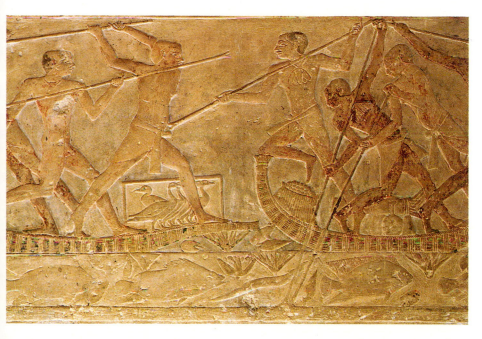

Representations of mock-fights among pole-wielding crews of papyrus-rafts returning from fowling expeditions are commonplace. The liveliness of the composition of such scenes is in marked contrast with the formality of the reliefs showing the tomb-owner.

grain in the Sixth Dynasty tomb of Ankh-mahor. 'I'll do as you like!' she says. 'Put your hand in this barley, it is still full of chaff!' a winnower rebukes her companion in the tomb of Ty.

The last stage, described in the tomb of Sekhem-ankh-ptah as 'measuring barley by the council', was carried out by the administrators of the estate: a 'crier' counting the number of measures of corn being stored in the granary, a 'scribe of the granary' recording it, and the 'overseer of the property' who was in charge of the farm, together with the 'keeper of the books of the official property'.

Ground emmer was used for baking many varieties of bread and cakes. Barley, wheat, and dates were the main ingredients for brewing beer.

Cattle-breeding, producing meat, milk, and hides, as well as providing draught animals, played a vital role in the economy of the Old Kingdom. The counting of cattle became the main part of the, initially biennial, and at the end of the Sixth Dynasty annual, census and taxation. An inspection of cattle is a common topic in tomb-reliefs. The vizier Akhtihotpe is accompanied by his eldest son and various officials while 'watching the cattle brought for the festival of the god Thoth from the estates of the spirit (*ka*) and the villages of the official property in Lower and Upper Egypt'. The 'estates of the spirit (*ka*)' were farms which supplied produce for Akhtihotpe's tomb. Herdsmen, some of whom are bringing calves or carrying bundles of fodder to induce the animals to move, are shown leading long-horned oxen (*gen* and *ren iwa*) decorated with large collars round their necks. These were animals to be slaughtered during the festival. The numbers of the inspected livestock are sometimes given; thus, in the Fifth Dynasty tomb of Rakhaef-ankh at Giza, they are 834 head of long-horned cattle, 220 head of hornless cattle, 2234 goats, 760 donkeys, and 974 sheep. Even for a well-to-do priest of the pyramid of Khephren these are very large numbers, and one may assume that they represent the holding of Khephren's cult establishment rather than that of an individual priest.

Parts of the Delta and elevated banks which separated the river from cultivated flood-basins were particularly suitable for grazing cattle. Herdsmen engaged in various bucolic activities often accompany marsh-scenes in tomb-reliefs. 'Herdsman! don't let that bull mount her!' is written above a representation of a man with a stick minding cattle in the Sixth

The hippopotamus was the fiercest and most powerful of the animals of the Nile, and the dangerous and exciting hippopotamus-hunt is sometimes shown in tomb-reliefs. The scene is usually just a cameo detail of a large composition, with the tomb-owner engaged in spearing fish or hunting birds with a throw-stick in the marshes. These were much more leisurely activities where the physical danger was reduced to falling off the papyrus raft. The hunting of hippopotami was an attempt to eliminate a potential danger to people and fields and, therefore, it cannot be properly described as sport. In this scene the prow of the papyrus skiff of the tomb-owner, Princess Sesh-seshet Idut of the Sixth Dynasty, is visible above the harpooned hippopotami.

Dynasty tomb of Khunes at Zawiyet el-Amwat. 'Hey! my darling, eat the bread!' a soft-hearted herdsman sitting on the ground beside a lying ox cajoles his charge on a relief in the Saqqara tomb of the vizier Ptahhotpe. Milking scenes occur, as well as depictions of cows suckling calves. 'Pull hard, herdsman, she is in pain!' an overseer commands in a calving scene where a cow with a swishing tail, a twisted head, and a bulging eye shows all the signs of distress.

Pigs were not represented in tomb-reliefs of the Old Kingdom. Attempts were made to breed, or at least keep in captivity, wild animals such as oryxes. This was caused by the traditional, by then outdated, requirements for certain offerings in the funerary cult, rather than by purely economic reasons. On one of the wooden panels which served as stelae (gravestones) in the Saqqara tomb of Hezyre, dating from the beginning of the Third Dynasty, 'sprinkling water', 'washing the hands', and 'burning incense', followed by 'wine', a stand with a bowl containing some unspecified food, 'a young oryx', and a joint of meat on a plate, are listed above the symbolic table with loaves of bread at which Hezyre sits.

Gardens supplied vegetables and fruit. 'Watering vegetable patches in

the garden of the official property by a gardener' is among the scenes in the Fifth Dynasty Saqqara tomb of Niankh-khnum and Khnumhotpe. A carefully prepared bed of lettuce, with small channels bringing water to each plant, can be seen in the tomb of Mereruka. Gardeners are watering the vegetables from pots which they carry on a yoke across their shoulders, while others are harvesting the crop. Onions or garlic are pulled up by a kneeling man on a relief from the early Sixth Dynasty tomb of Niankh-nesut. Cucumbers, leeks, beans, lentils, and melons were also grown.

Fruit-trees and vines were cultivated. A royal decree issued for Metjen, who lived in the early Fourth Dynasty and had it recorded in his tomb at Saqqara, granted him a 'land property 200 cubits long and 200 cubits wide, enclosed by a wall, equipped, and planted with useful trees; a very large pond is to be made in it, and fig-trees and vines are to be planted'. Such an orchard-cum-vineyard is represented in the Giza tomb of Iymery of the Fifth Dynasty. Two men are scaring away birds, while another two are climbing trees picking figs and some other fruit. The four most characteristic processes of viticulture come next: men picking grapes from vines trained on trellises, treading them in a crushing vat, pressing

must in a sack by twisting long poles attached to it, and finally filling wine-jars.

Figs and wine played the role of Egyptian food of the gods. The resurrected king is 'one of the four gods fashioned by the earth-god Geb, who traverse Upper Egypt and who traverse Lower Egypt, who lean on their staffs, who are anointed with unguent, who are dressed in red linen, who live on figs and who drink wine'. Dates were the most important among the other fruits, some only known by their names and as yet unidentified, which contributed to Egyptian diet during the Old Kingdom. Bee-keeping was practised, and a honey-harvest scene was among those in the sun-temple of Neuserre.

Groups of men netting fish and others trapping wild fowl were frequently represented episodes of life by the Nile. 'It is coming and it is bringing a good catch of fish!' exclaims one of the men heaving a large net which is alive with a variety of fish in the tomb of Ty. 'There are some good fish in it!' agrees his companion. 'What fishing, what a catch!' incredulously repeats one of the fishermen in the Fifth Dynasty tomb of Neferirt-nef. Reliefs show fish being cut open for drying and their roes extracted for the preparation of a relish (botargo), as well as being cooked on a spit over a fire.

Wild fowl was usually caught with large clap-nets. When the birds were enticed to settle down and feed on food scattered inside the net, it was closed with a rope pulled by men lying in wait. In the Sixth Dynasty tomb of Udjaha-teti at Saqqara the men, who have just vigorously closed the net and fallen over on the ground from the effort, tell each other with obvious pleasure: 'There are all kinds of catch in it!' In addition to catching wild fowl, there were also poultry-yards for breeding geese and ducks.

Bread and beer, supplemented by vegetables, fruit, and an occasional fish or fowl, with meat probably being an exceptional luxury, represented the diet of ordinary Egyptians. Offering-lists in Old Kingdom tombs give us some idea about the composition of the menu of upper-class Egyptians, but this was, no doubt, radically different from that of ordinary people in its range of food-items. Such a list appears above and in front of the table with bread-loaves at which Nikanesut is seated on a relief in his tomb at Giza. The list includes nineteen different kinds of bread and cakes, seven varieties of beer and two of wine, ten different cuts of beef, four species of fowl, seven types of fruit, wheat and barley, with onions as the only vegetable. Some of the entries in the list are repeated and probably represent varieties which were not further specified in the list, as in the case of wine, and so the number of items may be even higher.

Some of the foodstuffs produced by the farmers were used to satisfy their own needs. Much of the produce, however, was intended for the many temples and tomb-chapels serving the cult of the dead. The most spectacular of these were connected with pyramids. They represent the ultimate in Egyptian achievement in large-scale technology and organization. While, apparently, little attempt was made to distinguish the king's tomb by its size and form from those of his relatives and officials during

The old constructional principle of step pyramids, based on buttresses of masonry surrounding the central core, was retained even in true pyramids, and each of them thus contains a step pyramid inside its structure. These buttresses can be clearly seen on the tower-shaped ruin of the pyramid at Maidum. The Maidum pyramid was originally conceived as a step pyramid and subsequently modified to a true pyramid by additional casing, but the enormous pressures thus created were underestimated by its architect. This led to its partial collapse, though it seems that this did not happen until some time in the Middle Ages. The pyramid was originally built for the last king of the Third Dynasty and probably completed by Snofru.

The majority of cult temples (also called pyramid temples because they are adjacent to pyramids) have been almost completely destroyed as the result of the robbing of limestone for building purposes or for burning lime. The former practice started as early as the beginning of the Middle Kingdom, but the latter was rife from the Middle Ages to the middle of the last century. Sahure's temple at Abusir, although very severely damaged, provides even now a good idea of its plan and an inkling of its original decoration. The cult temples were built according to a well-established plan, and so they can be completely reconstructed, at least on paper.

the First Dynasty, we find the situation radically altered at the beginning of the Third. This impression of a sudden change is probably only illusory. The rock-cut substructures of the presumed royal tombs of the Second Dynasty at Saqqara have completely lost their brick-built buildings above ground, and if these reflected in any way the size of the galleries below ground, they would easily provide the missing link demonstrating the gradual increase in size in comparison with private tombs.

The ability to raise a large structure in stone appeared in Egypt at the beginning of the Third Dynasty. The earliest record of a stone building dates to the end of the reign of King Nebka, the first king of the Third Dynasty. One of his years in the 'annals' on the so-called Palermo Stone includes 'erecting [the building called] Men-netjeret in stone'. The structure has not yet been located. Shortly afterwards, a stone-built tomb was begun for his successor, King Netjerikhet, at Saqqara. It is not easy to be certain about the motive behind the departure in form from a mastaba, i.e. a flat-roofed tomb whose outside faces showed only a slight incline, to a stepped pyramid. It is possible that it was but a new presentation of an old concept. The core of some of the brick-built mastabas of the First Dynasty at Saqqara contained another superstructure in the form of a low and presumably truncated pyramid of many small steps above the burial chamber. This may have represented the original grave mound and been connected with the idea of the mythical mound on which life first appeared, while the mastaba's exterior, the niche façade, imitated the outward appearance of the royal palace. Mastabas of high officials, who at that time belonged to the royal family, and presumably also those of kings, thus combined a grave containing the body of the deceased with a dwelling for the continued existence of his spirit (*ka*). It would not have been uncharacteristic of Egyptian thinking to have preserved one within the other, and the fact that the concealed structure was not visible to human eyes was irrelevant. In the case of the step pyramid of King Netjerikhet both elements are present, but they are separated physically: the concealed mound is now freed and represented by the step pyramid, while the niche façade of the mastaba is now imitated by the niched enclosure wall of the whole complex.

The next significant change in the appearance of the royal tomb and its ancillary buildings occurred some seventy years later, at the beginning of the Fourth Dynasty. The innovations introduced at that time were so wide-ranging that they must have had their origins in the sphere of religion rather than technology. It is not improbable that other buildings, probably brick-built, were associated with step pyramids in the Nile valley, but none have been located so far. Pyramids of the Fourth Dynasty now had a monumental stone-built entrance (valley temple) at the edge of cultivation. This was connected by a causeway to a cult temple against the east face of the pyramid which stood in the desert. The cult temple was the main element of the now fully developed royal pyramid-complex, where daily rituals were conducted and token offerings presented to the spirit of the dead king. The pyramid was but a monumental sealed tomb which did not play a direct part in the maintenance of the cult. The pyramid-complex, the pyramid-town in the valley and its personnel, and the land and other possessions which constituted their economic basis, together formed the king's cult establishment.

At first, the cult temple had been situated to the north of the pyramid. Egyptian architects were, however, remarkably flexible and inventive in their approach to converting the demands imposed by religion into

Below left: Only one valley temple of the three pyramid-complexes at Giza, that of Khephren, can be visited. Khufu's valley temple is hidden under the houses of the village of Nazlet es-Simman to the east of the pyramid-plateau, and in view of the remarkable complete state of the rest of the complex its excavation sometime in the future offers a most exciting prospect. Menkaure's valley temple was unfinished at the time of the king's death, and the remains of its walls have, since its discovery, been once again covered by the sand. Khephren's valley temple impresses by the sobriety of its design, and is the best demonstration of the total dominance of straight lines—mostly at right angles—in Old Kingdom architecture.

Below right: The pyramid of Unas was the first in which the interior walls were inscribed with the Pyramid Texts. These inscriptions can be divided among some 750 utterances, or 2,300 shorter spells. Most of them appear in the six pyramids of kings and the three pyramids of queens, which contain the Pyramid Texts, but their selection and arrangement are not always the same.

reality. They were not afraid to improvise when forced to do so by circumstances: thus Userkaf's pyramid at Saqqara has its temple against its south face, presumably because of the presence of an earlier structure to the east, and the temple of Neuserre at Abusir was built off the central axis of the pyramid for the same reason. The changes in the orientation of the cult temple which took place in the Fourth Dynasty, accentuating the east–west axis of the complex, were of a different type and a more permanent nature. They were probably due to a modification of beliefs concerning the king's afterlife. The earlier notions of celestial voyages undertaken in the company of gods had been reflected in the predominantly northern orientation towards the north star. Now they were combined with the ideas about the kingdom of the underworld god of the west, Osiris, and confirmed by a western orientation.

One of the conspicuous features of ancient Egyptian mentality was the reluctance to abandon an old concept in the face of a new one. Combination of motifs and elements, and re-interpretation and syncretization of ideas were preferred. This was perhaps a reflection of a different approach to the notion of progress from that prevalent in modern societies. From the Fourth Dynasty on, the cult temple was regularly situated near the eastern face of the pyramid, but a small chapel continued to be built against the pyramid's northern face for the rest of the Old Kingdom.

The royal tomb itself changed its form from a step pyramid to a true pyramid at the beginning of the Fourth Dynasty. We have no solid evidence for the reasoning behind the change. It may have been the next logical modification to make in the development of the royal tomb, a true pyramid being the simplest and most perfect form which a structure with a rectangular ground plan can adopt, but it may have been an imitation of the summit of the obelisk associated with the sun-god Re of Iunu (Heliopolis). It was in the Fourth Dynasty, in the reign of Radjedef, that the royal epithets associating the king with Re appeared, and the name of the god now became a standard component of the king's *ni-sut-bit* name.

While each of the pyramids of the Fourth and Fifth Dynasties was of an individual design, all those of the Sixth Dynasty were, at least outwardly, of the same type: 150 by 150 cubits (78.75 metres, or about 250 feet) in ground plan, and 100 cubits (52.20 metres or 171 feet) high. Standardization was, as a rule, consciously avoided by the Egyptians, even though uniform tombs were built by Khufu for his family and officials at Giza. The state may have already experienced difficulties in undertaking large-scale projects, and pyramids of a standard size may have reduced the organizational problems. A pyramid of this size was still an impressive building, though modest in comparison with its predecessors, and would have simplified the planning decisions at the outset of the work.

The basic layout of the pyramid complex of the Fourth to Sixth Dynasties (valley temple, causeway, cult temple, pyramid) was imitated in sun-temples built during the Fifth Dynasty, and indicates that in the Old Kingdom there was a generally accepted concept of a purposefully designed and built temple. A large masonry obelisk (not monolithic) of the sun-temple served as the focal point of the upper temple. The open plan and decorative scheme stressed the beneficial influence of the sun-god and the ritual occasions of the reign, such as jubilee-festivals, sanctioned by him. Only two sun-temples, those of Userkaf and Neuserre, have so far been located with certainty and excavated, while another four, which are mentioned in texts, still await discovery.

Detailed information about the appearance of temples of local gods is almost completely lacking. With the possible exceptions of the temples of Re-Harakhti at Iunu (Heliopolis) and of Ptah at Ineb-hedj (Memphis),

The burial chamber of Ptah-shepses, the vizier of Neuserre, at Abusir. It contains a graffito which represents a method used by the stonemason to work out the measurements of the irregularly shaped lintel from data supplied by the architect. Egyptian geometry was entirely practical, and the author of the graffito was only as much a geometrician as a scribe adding and subtracting the number of bread-loaves in administrative documents was a mathematician.

the amount of royal building activities in these local temples probably remained limited throughout the Old Kingdom.

At Saqqara, royal tombs of the Second Dynasty and the step pyramids of the Third formed an isolated group some distance into the desert, with no tombs of lesser beings in their immediate vicinity. This was the concept of the original *ta djeser*, usually translated as 'sacred land', or 'necropolis', but which perhaps more accurately meant 'secluded region'. It was a continuation of the traditional arrangement of the earlier necropolis at Abydos. Non-royal tombs must have been built at some distance to the east, close to the valley. Such a strict separation of royalty and officialdom changed with the pyramid itself in the Fourth Dynasty. The area near the pyramid of the king now became crowded with tombs of members of the royal family, king's officials, priests, and craftsmen. The most prominent queens were buried in small subsidiary pyramids.

The king was at first deemed responsible for the provision of private tombs for the rest of the royal family and his officials. Snofru and Khufu carried out this duty in an exemplary fashion by laying out tombs for future use in a regular pattern in the neighbourhood of their pyramids as soon as space became available. The number of people who were able to secure a tomb in the royal necropolis grew, and the uniformity very quickly disappeared during the reigns which followed. Nevertheless,

Much of the stone required for building the Giza pyramids came from the vicinity of the site. This created a number of artificial rock faces which started in the reign of Khephren to be used for the complete or partial cutting of private tombs. Rock-cut tombs seem to have existed at northern Saqqara even earlier, so the idea was not new, but there natural rock cliffs were employed. Cost-saving was the main consideration. The tomb of Meresankh, one of the queens of Khephren, presents a combination of the rock-cut and free-standing techniques, with superstructure built over a rock-cut chapel. Some of the tomb features, including statues of the tomb-owner and relatives, were also cut in the living rock, and this method made the statues seem as if they were placed in niches.

proximity to the royal pyramid always remained an important consideration in the choice of the tomb-site for reasons of convenience and safety from depredations. While, with only one exception, the rulers of the Old Kingdom adopted pyramids for their burials, mastabas continued to serve as private tombs. It is possible that the first stone-built private mastaba at Saqqara was contemporary with the step pyramid of Netjerikhet, but it was not until the reign of Khufu that crews of royal workmen built them in large numbers at Giza. The earliest Giza tombs with rock-cut chapels, which opportunely used rock faces left after the quarrying of stone for pyramids, are only a little later, but even there Saqqara may have been in the forefront of development. Despite this, brick-built mastabas continued to be used for the rest of the Old Kingdom on account of their comparative cheapness and convenience.

To understand the formal development of the private tomb and its elements in the Old Kingdom, it is necessary to go back to the beginning of Egyptian history. Above ground, the mastabas of the First Dynasty were solid structures with the underground burial chamber inaccessible. The façade round these brick-built mastabas consisted of a series of niches imitating doorways ('palace façade') among which one, in the eastern face near the south-eastern corner, served as the focus for the posthumous cult. We can conjecture that this was the place to which offerings required by the spirit (*ka*) of the deceased were brought and where the ritual of presentation was conducted. A person standing outside the mastaba in front of this niche was facing west, the traditional Egyptian abode of the dead, and although we have no textual evidence from this early part of Egyptian history for this belief, already in the Predynastic Period most of

Individual private statues were by far the most common. Pair statues (man and wife, mother and daughter, etc.) and family groups were known, but really large groups were unique to statues cut in the living rock. This group of ten represents the women of Queen Meresankh's family at Giza, some probably shown more than once.

The pyramid-complex was surrounded by tombs which formed the pyramid cemetery. The workshops with craftsmen employed in the building of tombs and the maintenance of their funerary cults were located in the pyramid-town. There were precise reasons why a particular pyramid cemetery was chosen for the siting of a tomb. The tomb-owner may have served in the king's administration and the tomb or parts of it may have been royal gifts, or he may have been connected with the king's cult establishment. Family tradition and the place of origin were also of some importance. As a rule of thumb, it can be said that a man's tomb was built close to where his wealth and influence lay in his lifetime. Although of the Sixth Dynasty, Meryre-nufer Qar, who was 'overseer of the pyramid-towns of Khufu and Menkaure', and 'inspector of priests of the pyramid of Khephren', was buried in the old Fourth Dynasty cemetery at Giza.

the bodies were oriented towards the west. In the Second Dynasty a gravestone ('niche-stela') was placed at the back of this niche. In the Third Dynasty the niche developed into a small room approached by a narrow corridor, as if it had been withdrawn into the body of the mastaba for protection. This, indeed, was exactly what happened. A rudimentary one-room chapel was thus formed and the focus of the cult was now transferred from the outer face of the mastaba to the far wall of this chapel. The niche, formerly in the outer face of the mastaba, was now reproduced within the chapel itself. Such a transfer of function from one part of the structure to another without disturbing the underlying logic is characteristic of Egyptian thinking and can be observed time and again in burial customs. When the niche façade completely disappeared from outside the mastaba in the Second Dynasty, it re-appeared on the coffin which was also regarded as the house of the spirit (*ka*).

The fully stone-lined niche ('false-door' stela) was at first the only decorated feature of the chapel, but gradually reliefs started to take more and more space on its walls. The original single room within the body of the mastaba (though there may have been others outside) was added to until by the Sixth Dynasty virtually the whole superstructure was occupied in this way, thus in effect creating the semblance of a house. The burial chamber, which in the Old Kingdom was regularly at the bottom of a shaft dug in the rock substratum, was inaccessible, and it was only in the Sixth Dynasty that decoration extended there to even a limited degree. With the decrease in the number of large decorated chapels already becoming apparent, the burial chamber and particularly the coffin now took over some of the essential decorative elements of tomb chapels. When, during the general decline which followed the end of the Old

Kingdom, decoration virtually disappeared from tomb-chapels, it was only the false-door stela (i.e. the successor of the original niche in the façade) and the coffin which retained some of it, as if the cycle of development had been completed and only the essentials were left.

The original reason for the decoration of tomb-chapels was to provide the spirit (*ka*) of the deceased with the necessities of its continued existence in the after-life. On stelae of the Second Dynasty the tomb-owner is seated at a table above which is a list of offerings which could be read aloud if anybody wanted to make the 'presentation of offerings by voice'. As decoration extended to the walls of the chapel, some of the activities now shown in tomb reliefs were closely connected with the idea of provisioning, particularly the scenes of butchery. Others, depicting scenes taking place on the tomb-owner's estate or his household, represent an evolution of this concept: husbandry, netting fish and fowl, crafts, baking, cooking, brewing, and feasting. Other topics may have originally been of the same type, but now became traditional and perhaps were understood differently, e.g. the fowling and fishing in marshes. The tomb-owner is taking an active part in these scenes, rather than watching others as he does almost everywhere else. These activities may have been symbolic, and were not necessarily simple records of pleasure. Some of the scenes were included because they were associated with the main themes represented, though far from being essential: boatmen equipped with long poles are shown engaged in a jousting tournament beside netting fish, a flute-player accompanies reapers harvesting corn, and a pet baboon is 'helping' men pressing must by twisting poles attached to a sack of crushed grapes.

The tomb was built for eternity, and so it was a good place in which to record legal texts, particularly those concerning its endowment, letters

The chapel of the tomb of Meryre-nufer Qar was rock-cut; its mastaba-shaped superstructure, now lost, was stone-built. In the Giza necropolis such use of two different building methods was common. Some uniformity in the plans of tomb-chapels can be discerned during the Third and Fourth Dynasties, but later practically every tomb represented an individual combination of the prescribed tomb elements.

Khufu was the first to be shown with a hawk on his throne, but this, the only complete example of the genre from the Fourth Dynasty, belongs to Khephren. Made of greywacke, it is perhaps the finest Egyptian statue ever carved. The hawk-god Horus was closely associated with kings, and the bird of prey spreading his wings protectively around the king's head is a telling artistic expression of this idea.

received from the king, and autobiographical texts. Representations of funerals perhaps followed a pattern similar to that set by the decoration of temples by showing activities closely connected with the structure itself. As tomb decoration became varied, the craftsman/artist himself began to exercise greater personal influence over the selection of themes within the limits imposed on him by the purpose of the building.

The connection between reliefs and three-dimensional sculptures was very close. The style which can be observed in the art of the Old Kingdom had its roots in relief used in the court art of the late Predynastic Period. Sculptures in the round developed later. This is the picture obtained from excavated material, but the same sequence can be deduced from some of the characteristics of statues which show their origin in 'two-dimensional' relief. Already the earliest male standing statues invariably show the left foot advanced in the typically Egyptian 'flat-footed' posture. There are two reasons for this: the favourite 'main' direction in Egyptian two-dimensional art, as well as writing, was for figures and hieroglyphs to face right, while one of the basic representational rules was that none of the important elements should be obscured. For the Egyptians the ideas of completeness and perfection were almost identical. If we imagine two people of the same height, both facing right, represented side by side on the same base-line, it has to be the person farther away from us whose face is projected slightly forward of the face of the nearer person. If represented differently, the man's face, his most characteristic feature, would be obscured. In the case of the feet of a man standing facing right it is the left foot which is shown slightly advanced, even if the person is just standing, not striding. A sculptor started to make a statue by sketching its profile on a stone block from which he was going to carve, and thus introduced this element into three-dimensional sculpture.

Tomb-statues were deposited in *serdabs*, rooms made inaccessible to human beings for reasons of safety, but which were easily penetrable by the spirit. The statue's function as substitute abode for the spirit (*ka*) did not lead to attempts to produce a faithful likeness of the person in his or her tomb statues, because individuality was given them by the inscription of the tomb-owner's name.

The greywacke triads (groups of three) of Menkaure were found in the valley temple of his pyramid-complex at Giza. The king is shown accompanied by the goddess Hathor (with the sun-disc and horns), who was the patron deity of the valley where the temple was located, and by a personification of an Egyptian district, in this case Hu (Diospolis Parva). Menkaure's valley temple contained a series of such statues, but it seems that not all the districts were represented. This creates some problems when we try to explain their presence in the temple. It is likely that their purpose was similar to that of reliefs showing district processions in other pyramid-complexes. The statues are relatively small, around 95 cm (37 inches) high, and this invariably comes as a shock to those conditioned by monumental works of art of the later periods.

Royal sculpture was of a much higher standard than private sculpture, and produced a larger variety of types. Many royal statues were innovative, and while some set patterns which were imitated for the rest of Egyptian history, others were not to be seen again. There is little doubt about their individuality, resulting from the attempt to portray the facial features of the king, as well as from the stylistic peculiarities of the sculptors or their schools.

Radjedef was the first king, and apparently also the last, to be represented with a small figure of one of his queens squatting by his legs. In sharp contrast, a pair statue of Menkaure and his queen, probably Khamernebti II, standing by his side, is a study in dignity as well as affection. Both Radjedef's and Menkaure's sculptures served as the prototypes for many private statues of a husband and a wife.

Almost all statues were considerably less than life-size, and although colossal statues existed, they were quite exceptional. The material of royal statues varied greatly, with the more prestigious hard stone preferred, but even wood and copper were used. An entry in the 'annals' for one of the years of King Nebka of the Third Dynasty runs as follows: 'The year of: fashioning the copper statue called King Khasekhemui who is tall of the White Crown. The height of inundation on the fields: two cubits, six palms, two and a half fingers.' The sculpture was probably made of metal shaped by hammering and joined by rivets. Giving names to royal statues was a common Egyptian practice, and the episode shows that copper was still regarded as a very prestigious material. This sculpture has not been preserved, but similarly made statues of Pepy I and Merenre were found at Nekhen (Hierakonpolis).

Private statues were only very rarely made by sculptors capable of endowing them with individual features, even though we cannot always establish whether they are lifelike representations of their subjects. Some of the statues belonging to this category date to the Fourth Dynasty and were produced in royal workshops, e.g. the seated vizier Hemyunu dating to the reign of Khufu, or the bust of the vizier Ankh-haf, probably of the reign of Khephren. The apparent stagnation in the standard of private sculpture after the end of the Fourth Dynasty was because most statues were now ordered privately, and the ability of craftsmen available to a private individual was much lower than that of the top sculptors of the royal workshops who made some of the statues of the Fourth Dynasty.

The uniformity of types (seated, standing, scribe, and groups) was due to the fact that they were all tomb-statues, placed in *serdabs* and later in burial chambers, and thus performed identical roles. Several of them of different forms and materials may have been made for the same tomb. Private statues of the Old Kingdom are small, examples over fifty centimetres (twenty inches) in height being exceptional, and most of them were originally painted.

A greater variety occurred in the so-called servant statuettes. These were statuettes representing members of the tomb-owner's household performing various menial tasks, mostly connected with the preparation of food. Tomb provisioning, the same idea that inspired the earliest reliefs, must have led to the introduction of these sculptures in tombs.

Monumental architecture in stone is incomparably better known than domestic architecture in unbaked mud brick because its chances of preservation are much greater. Furthermore, continuous habitation in the cultivated area has largely obliterated traces of earlier dwellings. In the peasants' houses a corridor led to a rectangular walled open courtyard serving for a variety of purposes, such as a working area, a place for keeping animals, and probably also for cooking, with one or several

The earliest royal statue of the Old Kingdom was discovered in a closed room, serdab ('cellar' in Arabic), near the step pyramid of King Netjerikhet at Saqqara. The limestone statue is nearly life-size, and shows the king, enveloped in a tight-fitting cloak, seated on a massive throne, with his names inscribed on the front of the pedestal. The garment of Netjerikhet was the type worn during the jubilee-festival. Buildings erected for the festival were imitated in Netjerikhet's pyramid enclosure, and the festival was a frequent theme of decoration of royal temples. The present rather grim expression on the face of the king is due to the later plunderers of the temple gouging out the inlaid eyes.

roofed rooms at the back. The dwellings of settlers in the communally built 'pyramid-towns' present a surprisingly complex arrangement round a central court, with halls, bedrooms, a bathroom, and a storeroom.

The building of pyramids, temples, and tombs gave an enormous boost to the development of certain crafts, particularly those connected with the 'necropolis industry', but many of the products manufactured by craftsmen of the Old Kingdom were intended for everyday life. As before, metals worked were mainly copper and gold (or electrum). A metalworkers' shop, with various operations under way, is shown among the scenes on the walls of the causeway leading to the pyramid temple of King Unas at Saqqara. Electrum, an alloy of gold and silver, is the metal used by craftsmen in this scene, together with copper. Four kneeling men are cold-hammering the metal into sheets with stone hammers, while two of their colleagues are melting electrum in a crucible by blowing into long blowpipes in order to force the fire. The manufacture of metal vessels is shown next. One man is squatting on the ground either hammering a large bowl to shape over a wooden core or polishing it, and others are finishing a large vase and two spouted ewers and basins. The weighing of metal ingots and their recording takes place next to a metalworker with a blowpipe, perhaps casting the blade of an adze which his companion is shown sharpening.

Hammering remained the only method used to harden the cutting edge of cast tools. Copper implements found among the funerary equipment of Khufu's mother Hetep-heres I at Giza, perhaps unintentionally left behind by workmen, include a heavy chisel, a chasing tool ('punch'), and a knife in a decayed wooden handle. A copper ewer and a basin were found in the same tomb. The ewer was shaped by beating, but its spout was cast and fixed to it by cold hammering. Copper had its uses even in architecture. The drainage system of the pyramid temple of Sahure at Abusir employed hammered copper pipes, and a length of it was found still in situ when the temple was excavated.

Gold was cast as well as hammered. Sheet gold was used for covering objects made of wood, usually over a layer of plaster, and for plating other metals.

Carpenters and cabinet-makers manufactured a wide range of objects, in particular furniture and house-fittings, as well as items of tomb and temple equipment. On the relief in the Fifth Dynasty tomb of Ty at Saqqara a tall shrine, presumably for a standing statue, and a low chest on small legs, are being smoothed by two men with polishing stones (the plane was not known). This was the last stage of their manufacture, and most items being made by Old Kingdom craftsmen are shown like this, almost complete. A squatting man is shaping a plank with an adze, while another is vigorously sawing through a piece of timber attached in an upright position to a pole. 'Take another! It is hot!' is the advice given to him in the text concerning the large pullsaw. 'Polishing a bed of ebony by polishers from the official property' runs the description above two men busy with a bed, and 'a carpenter drilling a chest' above a kneeling man using a bowdrill.

Animal-legged beds, stools, and chairs, as well as chests and boxes, and also doors, door-bolts, and wooden columns for houses, and coffins and shrines for tombs and temples, were made by woodworkers. Axes, adzes, saws, bowdrills, and various chisels and mallets were the main tools used by Old Kingdom carpenters.

Several other crafts are shown next to metalworkers in the early Sixth Dynasty tomb of Ankh-mahor at Saqqara. Sculptors are busy carving and painting wooden statues. Four men are seated on the ground, each beside

The largest statue of the Old Kingdom is at Giza. The word sphinx may derive from Egyptian shesep ankh, *'living image', i.e. statue. The sculpture, some sixty metres (about 200 feet) long, represents a creature with the body of a lion, and the head of a king wearing the royal* nemes-*headcloth. The concept is the exact opposite of the usual way in which many deities were represented, with a human body and an animal's head. The idea of a lion guarding the entrance to a temple was known even earlier, and the sphinx at Giza was probably intended to protect the approach to the pyramid-complex of Khephren. The skill with which the two elements were combined is remarkable, as is the ease displayed in working on an unprecedented scale. There is no evidence that the sphinx enjoyed any form of worship in its own right during the Old Kingdom.*

The so-called reserve heads represent a curious and exceptional category of Old Kingdom sculpture. The prevailing concept that the human figure was shown unobscured and complete did not, apparently, apply to this series of limestone sculptures. As a collection of human types they are unparalleled in the Old Kingdom. There is every reason to believe that they are very realistically conceived, if not actual portraits, and one wonders whether this was connected with the fact that they are not inscribed. Although portraying officials, they must have been made by some of the best sculptors of the royal workshops of their time. Their purpose is perhaps summed up by the term 'reserve heads', and they may have been intended as substitutes should the tomb-owner's own head perish. The tomb in which this male reserve head was found is situated to the west of Khufu's pyramid at Giza, and dates from the middle or late Fourth Dynasty.

a stone vessel, two of which are being drilled and another two polished. The range and quality of stone vessels declined during the Old Kingdom in comparison with the preceding period, and they seem to have been chiefly used as containers for materials distributed from royal storehouses or traded with abroad.

On the same wall, three leatherworkers are manufacturing leather sacks and containers. One is making a skin more pliable by passing it over a wooden trestle, while another is cutting a piece of leather. Dyeing of leather was known. Sandals, various bags, sacks, boxes, and furniture fittings were made, with goatskins serving as containers for water, and rawhide was used for lashing blades of tools to their handles or hafts, or for joining parts of furniture. Skins of wild animals were worn on special occasions.

Jewellers complete the contingent of Ankh-mahor's workshop. Dwarfs were often employed in the manufacture of jewellery, and three pairs of them are shown here seated at low tables making a broad collar and two large collar counterpoises (*menit*). Similar items, also made of beads, are strung by jewellers in the register below. Scenes in other tombs show beads for such collars being drilled.

Pottery-making is only infrequently represented, the Fifth Dynasty mastaba of Ty at Saqqara being one of the few exceptions. A large pottery kiln is shown, with its minder squatting in front of it shielding his face from the heat, together with a man shaping a pot on a slow wheel, and several others finishing pots by hand.

Monumental building used up huge quantities of stone which had to be quarried and brought to the site. Most of the material was limestone quarried locally, preferably in the immediate vicinity of the building site. Limestone of better quality, used for the outer casing of structures and for lining the interior walls of tomb-chapels, came from the quarries at Roau (Tura), and had to be ferried from across the river.

Other stone used in building and making sarcophagi, altars, and statues travelled long distances: red and black granite from Aswan and Nubia, diorite from near Toshka in the southern part of the Western Desert, alabaster from Hatnub and greywacke from Wadi Hammamat, both in the Eastern Desert. These quarries were not opened permanently, but special expeditions were sent to them to bring material when it was required. A graffito at Hatnub, dated to the 'year after the sixth census' of Teti, mentions a force of 300 men taking part in such an expedition, while another may refer to as many as 1000 men. The leader of a quarrying expedition was usually described as 'treasurer of the god' (*sedjauty netjer*) and 'overseer of the task force' (*imy-ra mesha*).

Quarrymen and stonemasons were organized in the same way as the contingent of a boat. The largest unit was a crew (*aper*) of some hundred men which, for administrative purposes, had a name, such as 'Great', 'Pure', 'August', 'Satisfied', but apparently also 'Drunk'. This was usually connected with the name of the king for whom the crew worked. The crew was divided into five watches (*za*): starboard and port bows, starboard and port stern, and rudder, each consisting of two gangs of ten men.

Egyptian communications and transport during the Old Kingdom relied almost entirely on river and canal traffic. Large ships built of wood appeared when monumental building in stone began and the need for bringing large quantities of heavy materials to the building sites arose in the Third Dynasty. Egypt always was a country short of quality wood, and although local woods such as sycamore and acacia were used for small boats, timber had to be imported from the Lebanon and coastal Syria for the construction of large craft. Even these were built in the typically ancient Egyptian manner which showed that their ancestors were papyrus rafts, and so their hulls had no keel. Boat-builders working on smaller boats for everyday use are shown in a number of tombs. Small rafts were made of papyrus, but they were of limited life and carrying capacity, and so they were only used by peasants and herdsmen for crossing canals and marshy areas, or possibly by noblemen during fishing and fowling expeditions.

Even the heaviest stone elements could be transported in boats. In the reliefs of Unas' causeway, large monolithic palm-capital columns of Aswan red granite for the pyramid-temple of Unas are shown being shipped to Saqqara. The Egyptian artist cannot be entirely trusted to have accurately rendered the relative sizes of the boats and the columns, but the barges are described as 'laden with granite columns of twenty cubits', i.e. about 10.5 metres or 34 feet. Two columns are shipped in each barge, and so it appears that these must have been over 30 metres (100 feet) long. None of the barges has been preserved, though a ceremonial barque over 40 metres (134 feet) long has been found near the pyramid of Khufu at Giza. All valley temples of pyramid-complexes of the Old Kingdom were connected with the river by canals which, while the structures were being built, served as the main means of approach for all traffic. According to a fragment of an autobiographical text of an official responsible for transport it took seven days to cover the river distance of over 900 kilometres (600 miles) from Aswan to the capital.

The Nile is very suitable for river traffic, and there was no need to build special harbours or landing places. The granite region of the first cataract south of Aswan presented a natural barrier to boats and attempts to cut channels which would have enabled even larger ships to pass are known to have been made.

Egyptian sea-going ships displayed special modifications in comparison with boats intended for river traffic. The most significant of these was a cable connecting the bows and the stern above the deck, so-called hogging-truss, which provided a longitudinal support and thus compensated for the absence of a keel. Egyptian sea-going ability cannot be disputed, but it is likely that during these trips Egyptian ships were hugging the Levantine or Red Sea coast rather than venturing on high seas.

Although the concept of the wheel was known and employed for several purposes, roads in our sense did not exist during the Old Kingdom. Light loads were carried on donkeys along narrow tracks skirting the cultivated fields. Donkeys were also the only animals known to have been ridden. Wheeled transport did not exist. Heavy objects, almost exclusively building materials and funerary items such as stone sarcophagi, were transported on wooden sleds, dragged by cattle along sand- or mud-covered paths specially prepared to reduce friction. Only short distances were, as a rule, covered in this way, the only notable exceptions being mining and quarrying expeditions sent deep into the deserts, in which human force probably played the decisive part.

Donkeys were the only animals known during the Old Kingdom which could be used for long-distance expeditions, but their limited carrying capability and the need for bringing a supply of water for them imposed limits on the length of such trips. The 'overseer of Upper Egypt', Harkhuf, describes several expeditions to the southern land of Yam in his tomb at Qubbet el-Hawa during the reigns of Merenre and Pepy II. Three hundred donkeys made up his caravan during one trip, and the duration of two of these trips is given as seven and eight months.

There is no evidence in the form of texts for the state of astronomical and advanced mathematical knowledge during the Old Kingdom, but

The attitude of the Egyptians towards stone in architecture seems to have been quite different from their approach to sculpture. Statues of the most visually attractive materials were, nevertheless, often painted. On the other hand, for temples a judicious choice was made of contrasting colours of polished alabaster, basalt, granite and quartzite.

the precise orientation and the accurate measurements of buildings show the Egyptians' ability to solve the practical tasks involved in constructing monuments. Their approach to mathematical problems and their solution was, no doubt, entirely empirical rather than theoretical.

The Egyptian calendar was a practical consequence of astronomical awareness. A state like Egypt, with a sophisticated bureaucratic system, needed a calendar for advance planning and a reliable dating system. The calendar year had 365 days divided into three seasons of four months, each of thirty days, with five extra (epagomenal) days. In theory, New Year's Day coincided with the arrival of the annual inundation and so introduced the first season, *akhet*. The heliacal (pre-dawn) rising of Sirius after a period of invisibility also took place for the first time around this date. Two factors, however, made sure that all these events rarely occurred on exactly the same day. Firstly, the river did not start rising at the same time every year, and the variation could be considerable. Secondly, the calendar year was about a quarter of a day shorter than the astronomical year, and since no provision (such as a leap year) had been made to rectify the error, the calendar and the seasons were getting more and more out of step, at the rate of one month every 120 years. At the end of the Old Kingdom the difference, as compared with its beginning, was some five months, and the date expressed in terms of a season, month, and day of the civil calendar lost all relationship to the real season of nature.

While, at first, the various occasions recorded in the 'annals' were used to describe years, the choice of these eponymous criteria was eventually limited to the (mostly) biennial census of cattle. The year was 'of the n-th occasion of the census' or it was the year 'after the n-th occasion of the census'. Towards the end of the long reign of Pepy II the census probably became an annual affair or was abandoned, because shortly afterwards the designation of the year seems to correspond to the actual numbering of the regnal years of the king.

Like mathematics and astronomy, medicine relied on empirical rather than theoretical understanding. Many of the physicians (*sunu*) known to us from the Old Kingdom were attached to the royal palace and were thus members of the large retinue looking after the king's welfare. Some display titles which suggest that there was a degree of specialization, such as 'physician of the eyes of the Great House' (*sunu irty per-aa*), i.e. oculist. Whether this is a correct interpretation, or whether this is just a typically Egyptian way of converting totality into its constituent elements and presenting them separately (a physician dealing with all diseases could also be described as oculist, dentist, etc. depending on the particular problem he might be treating) is not certain.

Some medical works of later times were credited with great antiquity, but we do not know whether the attributions are genuine or whether they were just introduced to enhance their value. Medical instructions and precepts certainly were written down as early as the Fifth Dynasty. When the vizier Wash-ptah was taken ill in the presence of King Neferirkare, the king summoned royal children, lector-priests, and chiefs of physicians, and ordered containers with books to be brought and presumably consulted, though apparently in vain. The badly damaged record of this event was inscribed in Wash-ptah's tomb at Saqqara.

The extent of medical competence is not known to us because no medical texts of this early period have been preserved. Whatever empirical surgical knowledge existed, it could not have been acquired as the result of attempts at primitive mummification. The embalmers and physicians belonged to different specialized groups and there is no evidence of any connection between them.

After the beginning of the Fifth Dynasty, private statues were frequently competently made, and often pleasing in appearance, but rarely outstanding works of art. The wooden statue known as 'Sheikh el-Beled' ('Headman of the Village' in Arabic), found at Saqqara, is a happy exception, showing a corpulent ageing man with a remarkably expressive shrewd, rustic face. Even if the statue is a type rather than a portrait of an individual, it is the work of a master sculptor who was capable of transcending his role as a craftsman. The work dates from the end of the Fourth or the early Fifth Dynasty.

By the beginning of the Fourth Dynasty the hieroglyphic script, used in tombs and monumental inscriptions carved in stone, had produced the first longer texts. Earlier it was mainly used for descriptive notices identifying representations, and the names of officials on their stelae, and offerings systematically arranged into lists. The earliest type of text commonly used in private tombs was the 'offering given by the king' (*hetep-di-nisut*) formula. It was a short prayer asking the god of the necropolis, at first Anubis, for a share of reversion offerings which were presented to him by the king, but gradually it grew into a more complex system of wishes.

As the decoration of tomb-chapels began to occupy large areas of walls, some of the texts recorded snippets of conversation between the people represented. The first real narrative appeared as an autobiographical text in which the tomb-owner described events in his life. The emphasis in many of the early texts is on the official's possessions and how they were acquired, often with their description. The text thus represents a permanent record which should ensure that the tomb-owner's entitlement to these possessions is not forgotten. Parts of these texts may be direct quotations of legal documents.

In the Fifth Dynasty autobiographical texts developed further to include episodes illustrating the tomb-owner's character and describe his memorable achievements. These texts were, of course, idealized and never mentioned any failings. At the same time, a tendency towards formalization of the laudatory passages appeared. 'I am one beloved of all people. Never have I said anything wrong to the king or a person of authority about anybody. I am one praised by his father, his mother, and his lords in the necropolis,' claims Nekhebu in his tomb at Giza. 'I gave bread to the hungry, and clothes to the naked,' says Pepynakht Heqaib at Qubbet el-Hawa. On the one hand, the mere existence of these statements can perhaps be seen as evidence that behaviour described in them was not necessarily universal, but on the other they indicate a generally accepted moral code according to which a person was expected to live. The concern about complying with it suggests that one's prospects for afterlife would have been impaired by ignoring it. The concept of a moral evaluation was new, and perhaps the result of new religious ideas, particularly the increased importance of Osiris, which became widespread during the Fifth Dynasty.

Texts concerning the acquisition of the tomb are common, as well as threats to those found guilty of impropriety. Thus Akhtihotpe of the Fifth Dynasty at Saqqara claims: 'As for any people who enter this tomb of mine in an impure state, or who cause damage to it, judgement will be held upon them for it by the Great God.'

The incentive for the introduction and development of texts in tomb-chapels was thus closely connected with striving to ensure one's afterlife and the continuation of one's cult, and was not dissimilar from the motives which led to the introduction of tomb decoration and statues.

Unlike the monumental texts in tombs, the so-called teachings (*sebayt*) represent a purely literary genre transmitted on papyri. The form of these compositions is that of advice given by the father to his son as a series of maxims or instructions concerning his life and career. These works are a curious mixture of theoretical moral principles and of their very pragmatic application based on previous experience, and were intended for the select group of literate officials. The alleged author of the teaching invariably is a famous person, such as Prince Hardjedef of the Fourth Dynasty, or Izezi's vizier, Ptahhotpe, but whether these attributions reflect reality is not altogether certain. 'Do not be arrogant on account of what you

know, and do not be over-confident because you are a wise man, but consult the ignorant as well as the wise. The limits of skills have not yet been reached, and no expert is a complete master . . .'

Official monumental inscriptions did not substantially differ from the formally very accomplished administrative records in style and contents.

The Pyramid Texts represent the only large corpus of religious texts set down during the Old Kingdom. With the exception of the *hetep-di-nisut* prayer, private tombs contained neither religious texts nor representations of gods. Contact with the gods was the prerogative of the king.

The earliest uninscribed sheets of papyrus, the material used for every-day administrative purposes, were found in the Saqqara tomb of Hemaka of the reign of King Den of the First Dynasty. The manufacture of this type of writing material was fairly complicated and must have taken some time to perfect, but none of the earliest papyri have been preserved.

Most of our knowledge of the Old Kingdom comes from tombs. Though representations in tombs of wealthy Egyptians are concerned with their owners' needs in the afterlife, and with their funerary monuments, they record incidents which took place in this world. The picture derived from them may be selective, but it does reflect everyday reality.

Remains of the furniture found in the Giza tomb of Hetep-heres I, the chief Queen of Snofru and the mother of Khufu, included a bed, a bed-canopy, a curtain-box, two armchairs, a palanquin, and several chests. They have copper fittings, and their decoration consists of chased sheets of gold, and inlays in gold, carnelian, and faience. The furniture on display in the Egyptian Museum in Cairo has been completely restored using the original materials found in the tomb.

FIVE

MANAGING THE ECONOMY

'As for the villages of my tomb endowment which the king has given me for my provisioning . . . offerings presented by voice will come for me from them in my tomb which is in the necropolis of the pyramid called Khephren is Great . . .'★

WHILE ECONOMIC EXPLOITATION OF PROVINCES outside the capital Ineb–hedj by the central authority had remained at a fairly primitive level during the first two dynasties, rapid progress was made at the beginning of the Third. The village communities, which at first formed the basis of Egyptian agricultural production, were now systematically transformed. The control exercised by the state administrative system was strengthened.

The profound changes which took place were spurred on by the inauguration of monumental building in stone. The programme of pyramid-construction and the creation of the royal cult establishments associated with the pyramids shaped the society and economy of the Old Kingdom more than anything else. Such projects encouraged techno-logical and cultural advances and accentuated the differences between various sections of the community serving them. The pyramid was a material expression and affirmation of two of the basic tenets of state ideology and religion: the exceptional position and role of the king in the world, and the belief in continued existence after death.

It is customary to admire the unrivalled size and perfection of the massive structures raised at this early period of Egyptian history, but more impressive is the organizational and managerial genius of the men who were in charge of such enterprises, and their courage, imagination, and self-confidence in undertaking them in the first place. Large numbers of workmen were needed for handling stone blocks at building sites, and many more were engaged in their quarrying and transport, the building and maintenance of roads and construction-ramps, supply of workmen's tools, the care of draught animals, and provision of water, food, and other necessities of life. Many supervisors and scribes accompanied the labour force. Sculptors could only start their work on reliefs after the structures had been completed. The logistics of these operations must have been truly daunting. Even if much of the work which required a large work-force was carried out during the months of inundation when there was little to do in the flooded fields, the number of people whose provisioning

The burial chamber of the step pyramid of Netjerikhet, below ground level, was approached by a sloping shaft from the north.

★ *From a Fifth Dynasty text, now in Cairo Museum CG 1432, endowing a tomb at Giza.*

65

The appearance of large-scale building in stone at the beginning of the Third Dynasty accelerated changes in society as well as in arts and architecture. Seen from outside, Netjerikhet's enclosure walls imitated the appearance of the niched exterior of tombs of the First Dynasty, which themselves had probably adopted the exterior form of the royal palace. Engaged columns with the capitals in the shape of papyrus umbels were used in the heb-sed part of the enclosure. The step pyramid dominates the necropolis of Saqqara even now, and the enclosure walls as well as many of the buildings have been restored in years of painstaking research and work under the direction of J.-P. Lauer.

suddenly became the responsibility of the state was so large that the old system, geared towards the limited material requirements of the palace, could no longer cope unaltered. Most of the administrative changes which now started to take place in the organization of agriculture were due to the pressure to increase production.

From the beginning of the Third Dynasty new royal farming estates (*hut-aat*) were being created throughout Egypt. Many of them were founded during the reign of King Snofru, which saw an unprecedented increase in the volume of monumental building. An entry for one of his years in the 'annals' on the so-called Palermo Stone runs as follows: 'The year of: creating 35 estates with people and 122 cattle-farms; building a 100-cubit *Dua-taui* barque of conifer wood and two 100-cubit barques of cedar wood; the seventh occasion of a census; the height of inundation on the fields: five cubits, one palm, one finger.'

The monumental building of pyramids had a profound effect on Egyptian society and its economy. Cult and later also temple establishments now became an important element in the country's life. Their economic dependence on the central authority was gradually lessening. When royal cult establishments began to play a role in the material support of officials of state administration in the mid-Fifth Dynasty, it was an indication that the balance of economic power, based on land-ownership, had shifted very significantly. From then on these establishments represented a major economic force in the land, and acted as the main clearing houses for the distribution of national produce.

The king set out to prepare a pyramidal tomb for himself early in his reign, and also made legal arrangements for the theoretically indefinite maintenance of his posthumous cult in the temple adjacent to the pyramid. The main material requirement of a cult establishment was a guaranteed supply of provisions, such as bread, beer, meat, and fowl. Some of these were 'offered' to the spirit of the deceased king on the altar in the temple, while the rest was consumed by the temple personnel. Provisions came from various sources outside the temple. Remains of the papyrus-archive of the cult establishment called 'The *ba*-soul of King Kakai [= Neferirkare]' at Abusir show a high standard of book-keeping: 'Day 23. Brought from the Residence: 2 *des*-jars [contents not specified]; 4 jars of *zefet* [an unidentified liquid]; 1 loaf of *hetja*-bread; 2 loaves of *hetjat*-bread; 12 ducks. Brought from the storehouse of the valley estate [*ra-she*] of King Kakai: 3 *des*-jars; 1 loaf of *pezen*-bread; 1 loaf of another variety of bread. Brought from the chief physician Rakhuf: 1 duck.' On the following day, the 24th, exactly the same quantities of supplies were brought from the Residence. Other goods received that day were 'brought from the sun-temple called The Favourite Place of the Sun-God Re: 2 loaves of *hetja*-bread; 6 loaves of *hetjat*-bread; 2 loaves of *pezen*-bread, 1 cake, 10 ducks.' In each case the names of the men who came with these offerings were also recorded.

Not all provisions which were brought to the cult establishment remained there, because such an institution had its own 'clients' to whom it in turn re-distributed some of the offerings for use in their own tombs.

To safeguard his cult and make it economically independent, from the beginning of the Fourth Dynasty the king usually endowed his cult temple with land in the form of estates which then supplied it directly. Some of such land was in the valley not far from the lower part of the pyramid-complex, but most of the estates were situated in distant areas. Many of them were new foundations on territory previously unexploited, particularly in the Delta where free land was still available. To cultivate these estates peasants were re-settled from crown land elsewhere, to-

gether with cattle and equipment, and captives were brought from military campaigns abroad, particularly Nubia and Libya. The estates of Snofru's cult establishment are represented in the valley temple of his southern pyramid at Dahshur as a procession of peasant women, each carrying a symbolic tray with offerings. On their heads they have the hieroglyphic signs which read 'an estate of Snofru', and their names are written beside them. They are divided into groups preceded by the symbol of the district in which they were situated. This is a typically Egyptian device for presenting in a lively and visually attractive way what could have been a dry and rather dull copy of a systematically drawn-up legal document. Thus the standard of the Hare-district (the fifteenth of Upper Egypt) is followed by three such figures representing the estates called 'The Fishing Net of Snofru', 'The *pak*-bread of Snofru', and 'Snofru is Great'. The standard of the Oryx-district (the sixteenth of Upper Egypt) introduces a group of five estates, 'The Joy of Snofru', 'The Dancers of Snofru', 'The Road of Snofru', 'Snofru is Luscious of Pastures', and 'The Nurse of Snofru'.

In the second half of the Fifth Dynasty a noticeable increase in the occurrence of titles connected with pyramids shows that cult establishments had become an inseparable element of the central economic management of the country. Previously the personnel, supervised by an 'overseer of the pyramid' (*imy-ra mer*), had consisted of a lector-priest

The pyramid at Maidum represents the transitional stage of development from the step pyramid enclosures to the full pyramid-complexes. The valley of the complex, however, has not yet been excavated, and so we do not know whether there was a pyramid-town near the valley temple.

Inspection of cattle and fowl, including cranes, in the Fifth Dynasty tomb of Ty at Saqqara. The restored slit-aperture is one of three connecting the offering-room with the sealed serdab (statue-room) beyond.

who conducted the daily ritual, and his assistants, 'part-time' priests called *waeb* ('pure one') or *hem-netjer* ('servant of the god'). They had been organized into five 'guilds' (*za*) which served monthly in turn. The names of these 'guilds' were adopted from ship terminology. When not on duty, the priests had been craftsmen, cooks, farm-hands, and other skilled or semi-skilled workers who lived in the 'pyramid-town'. This was a settlement which had grown in the valley near the monumental entrance (valley temple) to the pyramid-complex. The social status of such people had hardly been elevated. Now, however, even the highest officials of administration began to hold offices connected with pyramids. Thus the vizier Akhtihotpe, who lived at the end of the Fifth Dynasty, is described in a scene in his tomb as 'chief justice and vizier, overseer of the broad hall, king's chamberlain, *iun-kenmut*-priest, judge and *adj-mer* official, priest of the goddess Maet, and overseer of the two towns and inspector of the two pyramids called Djedkare is Beautiful, and Menkauhor is Divine of Cult-Places'. It may have been the increased shortage of unexploited land which made the king use his cult establishment to support his officials or to provide for their tombs. A formal appointment to a 'salaried' nominal priestly function in such an establishment carried with it entitlement to income in kind from the temple's resources, or to the use of some of the temple's land in the form of one or more estates. These became one of the

Left and below left: A procession of semi-divine personifications, from Sahure's cult temple at Abusir, is led by the Lower Egyptian Hapy (representing fertility), and includes Nekhbet (meaning 'budding', not connected with the goddess Nekhbet) and Wadj-wer ('great green', probably meaning 'mass of water').

Below right: Food articles brought to tombs include fish. There is no doubt that they were eaten, at least by ordinary people, yet they are not listed among the standard offerings. This must have been due to prohibitive religious precepts according to which fish was not 'pure' food. The offering-bearers shown here conclude a long procession of personifications of the estates of Nefermaet. His early Fourth Dynasty tomb is at Maidum.

71

The slaughtering of oxen or oryxes is shown in almost all tomb-chapels, but these are provisioning scenes which do not necessarily reflect everyday reality. Meat was a prestige food which the peasantry could hardly afford. This relief is in the Sixth Dynasty tomb of Princess Sesh-seshet Idut at Saqqara.

possible forms of the appointee's official ('ex officio') property for life, but had to be surrendered by his heirs. With each new pyramid a large area of cultivated land inevitably ceased to be directly available to the central authority, but this measure now meant that at least some of it was in fact used twice, as a donation to the royal cult establishment, and also for the support of the king's officials.

Two of the fourteen estates listed in the Fifth Dynasty tomb of the official Nen-kheft-ka at Saqqara were called 'The Ladder of Userkaf' and 'Userkaf is Beautiful of the Spirit', while another three were 'Hathor wishes that Sahure lives', 'The Spirit belongs to Sahure', and 'The Flood of Sahure'. Nen-kheft-ka's claim to these estates as his official property was, no doubt, due to the fact that, as his titles show, he was associated with the pyramids of Userkaf and Sahure in nominal priestly capacities.

The inroads into state resources made by the creation of royal cult establishments were deepened even more by the practice of issuing protective decrees which dispensed their members from taxation and state forced labour. Such a decree was made out in the year of the twenty-first census by Pepy I for 'the cult of the King of Upper and Lower Egypt, Snofru, in the two pyramids called Snofru Appears. The Majesty of Horus Merytaui [= Pepy I] ordered for him [i.e. Snofru] that this pyramid-town be exempt from carrying out any work of the administration of crown property and from paying any tax of any tax-department of the Residence, and from any forced labour of any department of forced labour, no matter who says so'. The decree then details possible demands which could be made on the inhabitants of the pyramid-town and specifically prohibits their imposition on this cult establishment.

During the Sixth Dynasty even very high officials were proud to display the humble title of 'settler' (*khenty-she*) of their king's cult establishment. Meryteti, the son of the vizier Mereruka and himself a vizier under King Pepy I, had the following titulary inscribed on the left side of the door to his tomb-chapel at Saqqara: 'Inspector of servants of the god of the pyramid called Meryre is Established and Beautiful, settler, king's son, count, sole companion.' The title of the 'king's son' was, of course, only honorific and bestowed on him in order to enhance his court rank. The greatest benefit derived from the title of 'settler' may have been exemption from various state obligations which the holder now enjoyed as a member of the royal cult establishment.

The complex arrangements made for the posthumous cult of kings were paralleled, albeit on a much smaller scale, by those in the privileged sections of society. The king's unique role carried with it an obligation to ensure the maintenance of the funerary cult of his officials and members of the royal family. The requirements were twofold: building the tomb, and supplying the necessary offerings and provisions. Graves of the vast majority of ordinary people continued to be dug in cemeteries on desert margins as before, and remained unaffected by the cult provisions made for the upper echelons of society.

At first, all tombs situated within the limits of the royal pyramid cemetery were probably built and provided as the king's favour by royal craftsmen. 'As for this tomb of mine, it was the King of Upper and Lower Egypt Menkaure—may he live eternally!—who ordered it to be made, when royal progress to the pyramid plateau took place in order to inspect the work done on the pyramid called Menkaure is Divine, with the royal architect, the two chief directors of craftsmen, and craftsmen in attendance on him, so that he could inspect the work on the building. Fifty men were detailed to work on it every day and assigned to prepare

The plan of the tomb-chapel of Ptah-shepses at Abusir includes a large pillared court. The centre of the court was open to the sky, but the now fallen architraves supported slabs which formed a roofed walk round its perimeter.

73

The division of the economic resources available for the maintenance of the funerary cult was reflected in the size and quality of the tomb, even though turning this into a simple equation cannot be justified. The people who could use their position in life to provide themselves with large and splendidly decorated tombs were not necessarily only those who held the most important offices in the state administration. Nor can we link increases or decreases in the sizes of tombs directly to the importance of the office. The mastaba of Neuserre's vizier Ptah-shepses dominates the whole necropolis at Abusir by its size and its architecture.

the purification tent of the place of embalmment. His Majesty ordered that none of them be taken away for any task except working on it until it was completed.' The damaged inscription mentions further 'bringing stone from the quarries at Roau in order to encase the building in limestone, and two jambs of the doorway to this tomb'. The rock-cut tomb of Debehni, whose construction is described in this text, can still be visited north of the causeway leading to the pyramid of Menkaure at Giza.

From the Fourth Dynasty onward, private enterprise started playing a significant role in tomb-building. 'The necropolis-workman Pepi is satisfied with the contract which I made with him', proclaims the treasurer of the royal granary Neferher-en-ptah on the lintel of the entrance to his tomb at Giza, dated to the Fifth or Sixth Dynasty. 'I had these statues made by the sculptor who is satisfied with the reward which I made him,' says the priest Memi in the inscription on one of the two statues found in his tomb at Giza. The craftsmen employed in the construction and decoration of the Saqqara tomb of Hetep-her-akhti 'made it for much bread, beer, cloth, oil, and barley', while Metjetji, of the end of the Fifth or the beginning of the Sixth Dynasty, claims about everybody who worked in his tomb: 'I made them satisfied—after they had completed the work on it—with copper belonging to me from my official property, while I also gave them cloth and fed them with bread from my official property.'

Tombs were provisioned in several ways which developed historically and often existed simultaneously. Supplies of offerings could be received from a royal property or a royal cult institution as an 'offering given by the king (*hetep-di-nisut*). The practical disadvantages of this method were considerable, and so from at least as early as the beginning of the Fourth Dynasty there is evidence for the 'offering given by the king' taking the form of land endowments. In its purest form (*hut-ka*, 'estate of the spirit') such an endowment consisted of an estate with land, people, cattle, and equipment, which was given outright to the tomb-owner to provide the required necessities for his tomb. A third method of securing offerings for the tomb was by 'reversion' (*wedjeb*) of provisions from royal cult or temple establishments or other tombs. Some of the revenue received by

74

the original institution, in the most extreme case a tomb, was reverted, or re-directed, to be used as offerings in a secondary tomb. This was a characteristic way of legally arranging for the sharing of produce among several recipients, and one which can be seen in many forms at various levels of Egyptian society. A text in the Saqqara tomb of Persen, dating to the early Fifth Dynasty, provides an example: 'Bringing offerings for a presentation by voice, to the inspector of the Great House, Persen, consisting of reversion offerings of *hetja*-bread, *pezen*-bread, and *zefet* [an unidentified liquid], which come from the temple of Ptah South-of-his-Wall for the King's mother Neferhetpes daily eternally—given to him from it for a presentation of offerings by voice in the time of King Sahure.' Some of the revenue which the tomb of Queen Neferhetpes received from the temple of Ptah in the capital was reverted for Persen's own posthumous cult, perhaps because of a position he held in the queen's household. Such a re-distribution of offerings could take place several times over, because the tomb-owner could revert some of the income of his tomb yet again for use in tombs of his subordinates and lesser members of his household. This is the concept underlying the term *imakhu*, 'one provided for'. A man became *imakhu* by being promised a share of the offerings received by a god (i.e. from a god's temple) or a king, but also of those received by an important official or a member of the royal family with

whom he was in some way connected. Netjer-punesut is in his tomb at Giza described as the 'possessor of provisioning' from Kings Radjedef, Khephren, Menkaure, Shepseskaf, Userkaf, and Sahure. At the end of the Old Kingdom a lowly official Khuen-ptah claimed to be 'one provided for by the hereditary prince Meri', thus indicating that he enjoyed, or hoped to enjoy, the privilege of receiving a share of offerings from the large Saqqara mastaba of the vizier Mereruka (Meri was his nickname) in whose vicinity he was buried. It was common practice during the Old Kingdom for the tomb-owner to describe himself as 'provided for by' the gods of the necropolis, such as Anubis or Osiris, or by 'his lord', i.e. the king. A woman could be 'provided for by her husband'. These cases, wishful epithets without any legal force, are yet another reflection of the Egyptian approach to personal dependence and patronage.

In the tomb, food and drink offerings were placed on a special stone table or in a basin in front of a stela (gravestone) which resembled a door with several sets of jambs and lintels ('false-door'), and the ceremony of 'presentation of offerings by voice' was then conducted by a lector-priest. If the tomb was endowed with its own land (*djet*), the people who worked on it were legally tied to it. They assisted in the tomb ritual and so were described as 'servants of the spirit' (*hem-ka*) and 'belonging to the endowment' (*ny-djet*).

If the tomb had no personnel of its own, 'servants of the spirit' could be hired in return for contractually specified benefits, often the use of land, though not its ownership. The eldest son and heir was usually in charge of the affairs of his father's tomb endowment, so that control over the

property remained in the same family, but it could be the widow who took control if there were no children. A 'brother of the endowment' (*sen djet*), in effect a professional manager, was appointed in the absence of a next-of-kin.

With the exception of the temple of Ptah in the capital, the temple of Re-Harakhti at Iunu (Heliopolis), and the sun-temples, there were few religious establishments whose economic importance matched their spiritual significance before the middle of the Fifth Dynasty. Donations made by the king for the maintenance of ritual in these temples could take the form of produce delivered from state storehouses or estates. A list of offerings presented to the sun-temple of King Neuserre at Abu Ghurab on the occasions of various religious festivals was inscribed on its gate and probably represented a copy of a document lodged in the royal archive. The list is, unfortunately, preserved in a very fragmentary state. For New Year's Day festival the offerings included loaves of *pezen*-bread, and also milk and honey. For the 'coming out', i.e. public festival procession, of the god Min the temple received 1000 loaves of *pezen*-bread, one ox, ten geese, honey, *sekhet*-grain, wheat, and 'all sweet things'. The annual total at the end of the list amounts to 100,800 'rations' consisting of bread, beer, and cakes, 7720 loaves of *pezen*-bread, 1002 oxen, 1000 geese, etc. Whether these figures include the offerings presented on special occasions, or whether they represent daily offerings, is not clear, but they do show the large quantities of food which passed through a single temple in a year. These products were not 'wasted' as offerings for the sun-god, but were consumed by the temple personnel and often re-distributed elsewhere.

An unusually eroded alabaster block can be seen in the middle of what used to be the pillared court in the eastern part of Teti's cult temple at Saqqara. It is all that remains of a large altar decorated with the king's names and personifications of Egyptian districts. Whether this particular altar was functional, or just symbolic, is not clear. We can be more certain about the purpose of another, similar, altar. This is now lost, but originally it stood in the inner, western, part of the temple, and offerings required in the funerary cult of the king were brought there and placed on it in front of the stela (false-door).

More important factors in Egyptian economy were donations of land made to these temples. The area of the land presented in this way could vary very considerably from one donation to another. According to the 'annals' on the Palermo Stone, the goddess Hathor, whose cult was connected with the valley part (ra-she) of the pyramid-complex of King Sahure at Abusir, received just over two arouras (setjat) of land, about half a hectare (about 1.2 acres), in the year following Sahure's second census. The god Re was given over 1704 arouras, i.e. nearly 470 hectares (1161 acres), as one single donation in the year after the third census of Userkaf. During the Fifth Dynasty such donations were made on a larger scale even to provincial temples. As a result, many officials in local administration benefited greatly from the priestly offices they held in their local temples, and this significantly strengthened their growing economic independence of the central government. The increasing number of tombs in the provinces towards the end of the Old Kingdom testifies to this trend, but did not reflect a tendency towards political autonomy.

Most of the land which did not belong to any of the numerous royal cult and temple establishments and tomb endowments, and which was not cultivated as official property by private individuals, was administered by the state as part of 'crown property'. This land was managed by the Residence (khenu), which also directed fiscal affairs and so concentrated most state income in its hands. Only a very limited area of land may have remained private, of either individuals or the remains of the original village communities.

Manpower required for a limited period of time for large building, quarrying, and other projects organized by the state was drawn from all people throughout the land. Only those who were exempt from state forced labour (wenwet or kat) by special royal decrees were able to escape this burdensome obligation. In this way the administration also raised temporary help with agricultural tasks, such as cattle-herding, on royal estates which suffered from shortage of manpower. A decree, issued for the temple of the god Min at Gebtiu (Koptos, modern Qift) by Pepy II in the year after the eleventh census, prohibits imposition of such duties on the temple's personnel: 'My Majesty does not allow: that they are put to work in cattle-pens, on farms of cattle, donkeys, and small cattle [i.e. sheep and goats] of the administration of herds, or any forced labour or any tax which may be imposed by crown property administration for the length of eternity.'

Taxation (medjed) in kind was directed towards institutions rather than individuals. The census of cattle was the most regular and comprehensive method which covered the whole country, but there were other forms, some perhaps of an occasional nature, which varied according to local conditions. When the decree of Pepy I, issued for the cult establishment of Snofru at Dahshur, exempts it from 'counting canals, ponds, wells, shadufs, and trees', we must assume that these served as criteria for tax-assessment.

The king's responsibility for supplies of provisions for the tombs of his officials and members of the royal family was only an extension of his obligation to provide their necessities in their lifetime. At first all important positions were held by members of the royal family who, because they themselves did not work on the land, received provisions directly from the royal palace. This was no longer possible when administration became more complex and covered all Egypt. A new and more efficient method of provisioning was based on assigning some crown land to royal relatives and officials for their use. The person owned this land, usually with people and cattle, for his lifetime. It was his official ('ex officio')

A new type of stela was introduced in the stone-built tombs which King Khufu built for his officials and royal relatives. Called slab-stelae for their shape (more wide than high), they were made in royal workshops and presented to the tomb-owner by the king, so they display an excellent standard of workmanship. They were only used at Giza for a limited period of time. This stela belonged to Princess Nefertiabt.

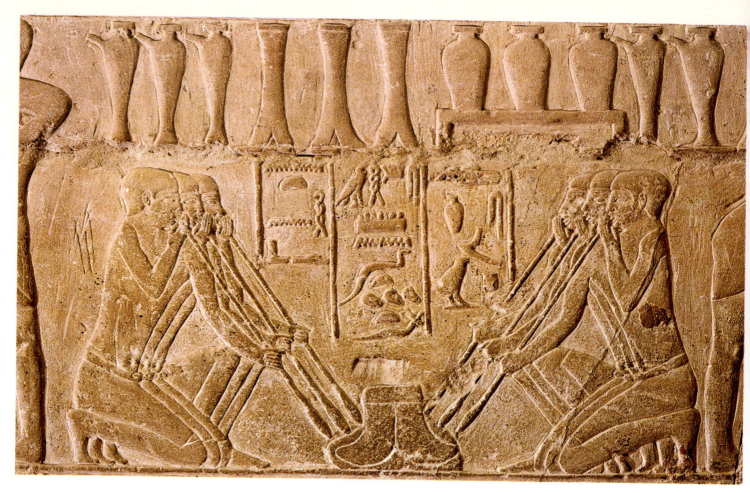

Craftsmen shown in the early Sixth Dynasty tomb of Mereruka at Saqqara include metalworkers and dwarfs employed in the manufacture of jewellery. To force the fire, metalworkers used blowpipes during the melting of metal in order to transform the mass extracted from the furnace into ingots.

property (*per-djet*) and represented his 'salary', but he was also expected to use it to maintain his large household and his professional subordinates, and thus to act on the king's behalf in supporting them. A direct grant of land represented the original form of official property, and members of the royal family particularly benefited from it. The same end was often achieved by appointing officials to nominal positions connected with royal cult establishments or estates of crown property, which then entitled them to such official property.

A man's private property thus usually came from several sources. In a scene in the late Sixth Dynasty tomb at Deir el-Gebrawi the owner, Ibi, describes how he has assembled provisions for his tomb: 'I have created it from the villages of my official property (*niuut djeti*), from my priesthood, from the 'offering given by the king' which the Majesty of my lord gave me so that I might acquire for myself fields . . . settled with the people of the endowment, furnished with cattle, goats, donkeys, and that which I acquired by my own arm—beside the property of my father—while I was manager of an estate of crown property [*per shena*] of 203 arouras of land which the Majesty of my lord gave me to make me wealthy.' Much of Ibi's accumulated possessions came from his appointment as manager of a royal estate, but a contribution was made by the income from his priestly office, an 'offering given by the king', and some property which he inherited from his father. 'That which I acquired by my own arm' may refer to property which was purchased by him. Such cases are not common, but occur already in the early Fourth Dynasty.

An illustrated version of the title deeds to one's estates was often represented in the tomb as a procession of women bringing offerings or leading animals. This was a method similar to that used in temples associated with pyramids. The nouns 'estate' and 'village' are of feminine gender in Egyptian, hence the sex of these offering-bearers. Meresankh, one of the queens of Khephren, had thirteen estates recorded on the east wall of her Giza tomb: one 'estate of Khufu' (*hut Khufu*), i.e. a farm newly created by the king, which she received because she was his granddaughter, ten villages of Khephren which she was given by her husband, one village of Radjedef whose presence can be explained by the fact that Radjedef was her stepfather, and one 'estate of the spirit' (*hut-ka*). The last estate constituted her tomb endowment and was to provide offerings for her tomb, in theory for ever, while the rest had to be surrendered after her death.

Three estates are shown in the Saqqara tomb of Metjen of the early Fourth Dynasty. One is called 'The Endowment of the Ram of Mendes', and probably represented Metjen's official property, but the other two are described as 'foundations of Metjen' called 'One who Comes when she Wishes' and 'The Mound of the God Sobek'. The mention of the tomb-owner in their names suggests that, unlike the first estate, these were specially created for Metjen and thus constituted his private inalienable property which he was allowed to dispose of in his will as he wished.

It is possible that some of these private estates represented in tombs did not belong to the tomb-owner exclusively, but rather supplied him only with some particular produce. This may explain some of their names, for example in the Fifth Dynasty tomb of Ty at Saqqara: 'The Wine of Ty', 'The Milk of Ty', 'The Fig of Ty', and others. These estates may even have been completely fictitious, but the evidence of tomb reliefs, unfortunately, is not detailed enough to enable us to distinguish such subtleties.

The Old Kingdom approach to the provisioning of the living and the methods used to achieve it were thus not unlike those for the provisioning

Part of the will in which Kaiemnefert endows his tomb in the necropolis of the pyramid of Khephren during the Fifth Dynasty. Kaiemnefert had the title of the 'adj-mer manager of the estate called Star of Horus Foremost of Heaven', a vineyard in the Delta. It is, however, certain that this prestigious ancient title had become purely honorific by the Fifth Dynasty. The stone block was originally set up in Kaiemnefert's tomb at Giza.

Facing page: The exquisite low reliefs from King Userkaf's cult temple at Saqqara include some lively swamp scenes, perhaps connected with fishing and fowling. Although Userkaf also built a temple for the sun-god at Abusir, there is nothing to suggest that the state's economic resources were unduly strained: the quality of this work is very high.

of gods or the spirits of the dead. Despite different ideological motivation, they all represented means of securing distribution of the surplus national product among the privileged section of society in the most desirable way.

Internal trade had only a limited role to play in the country's economic life during the Old Kingdom. Peasants produced most of what they needed for themselves, and received other necessities, such as certain items of food (fish, fowl, salt, honey, oil), clothes, sandals, and perhaps some house fittings and furniture, from the owner of the land on which they were settled. Craftsmen were provisioned by the institutions for which they worked. Officials lived off their official property, mostly state land they were allowed to use in return for their services, or received goods directly from the state. Only a small amount of surplus produce was distributed through village markets, and apart from barter scenes in tombs there is no evidence to show how this worked.

Buying and selling of private property was a legally recognized practice which was recorded in documents. A few of these transactions are known to us in detail because, quite exceptionally, the records were copied on to stone. Tombs and their elements, including statues, as well as fields for one's tomb endowment, could be acquired by purchase, but also everyday necessities such as a house. 'I have bought this house from the scribe Tjenti. I gave him the value of 10 *shat* for it: four-strand cloth to the value of 3 *shat*, a bed of sycomore or jujube wood of the value of 4 *shat*, and two-strand cloth to the value of 3 *shat*.' There was no money as

such, and payment for goods and services was made in kind, and could
thus be described as exchange. The term *shat* employed in Tjenti's document seems to represent a fixed official unit of value, expressed in terms of
an amount of metal, in which transactions were calculated.

Egypt was almost completely self-sufficient in natural resources and
most of the materials and products obtained through foreign trade
belonged to the category of prestigious luxury goods. Timber from the
Lebanon and Syria was the major exception. Commodities such as lapis
lazuli, wine, and oils came from or through the same region, with Byblos
playing an important role in maritime trade. Reliefs from the pyramid-
temple of Sahure at Abusir show the return of Egyptian sea-going ships
from such an expedition, bringing back bearded Asiatics who are represented as making obeisance to the king. A similar scene was also identified
at the causeway leading to the pyramid of Unas at Saqqara. Whether these
are records of actual events, or a genre of no historical relevance, is not
clear, and we do not know the purpose of these expeditions. Tall-necked
jars, presumably of oil, and bears, exotic animals for the Egyptians, are
shown in Sahure's temple and may be connected with the trip to Asia.

Overland routes must have also been used.

Caravan routes remained the main links with the African regions lying beyond Nubia, which were the source of incense, hard woods such as ebony, oils, ivory, skins, ostrich feathers, and gold. Journeys to the land of Punt, probably situated inland from the Somali coast, were undertaken via the Red Sea. An entry in the 'annals' on the Palermo Stone for the 'year after the seventh census' of Sahure mentions the commodities 'brought from Punt', which included 80,000 measures of myrrh, 6000 units of electrum, 2900 units of wood, and 23,020 measures of unguent. The official Khnemhotpe recorded in the Sixth Dynasty tomb of Khui at Qubbet el-Hawa that he went with Khui and Tjetji, the 'treasurers of the god', to Punt and Byblos several (the figure not clear) times. A dwarf brought from Punt by the 'treasurer of the god' Werdedba in the reign of Izezi is mentioned in the letter of the young Pepy II to Harkhuf.

Egyptian exports seem to have been mostly manufactured goods, and included faience and stone vessels, probably filled with oils, and also clothes and furniture.

SIX

SOCIETY AND STATE

*'The order is great, its effectiveness endures. It has not been disturbed since the time of Osiris.'**

Alabaster was less commonly used for private sculptures, and the quality of the modelling of this statue is far above most Old Kingdom private works. It seems likely that it was produced in a royal workshop at the end of the Fourth or early in the Fifth Dynasty, and the woman may have been a king's relative or the wife of a high official. The exact provenance of the piece is not known.

THE SIZE OF THE EGYPTIAN POPULATION during the Old Kingdom is not known, but an estimate of about a million inhabitants, giving a relatively low population density, would probably not be far off the mark. Essentially it consisted of two main groups: the mass of peasants who worked on the land which they did not own, and the limited number of people broadly described as titled officials, who enjoyed the direct or indirect possession of land through one of the many forms which land-ownership could take. With the passing of time, craftsmen, particularly those belonging to royal cult establishments, emerged as a recognizable section of society because of the special status and privileges granted to them. Members of the royal family soon became, for ideological reasons, a group apart from the officials, as well as from the rest of the population. The apparent similarities to the situation of the late Predynastic Period and the first dynasties, with its division between the ruling *paat* related to the king, and the *rekhyt*, ordinary populace, would be misleading. The position of the king was, according to Egyptian state doctrine, quite exceptional, but other members of the royal family ceased to take an active part in the running of the state during the Fifth Dynasty and were relegated to supporting roles in the sphere of state ideology.

The king's relationship to gods (*netjeru*) was directly reflected in some of his names and titles. He was identified with the hawk-god Horus by the first and most ancient of his five names, related to the protective goddesses of Egyptian kings called Nekhbet and Wadjet ('The Two Ladies') by the second, and declared a 'son of the god Re', i.e. his heir, by his fifth name. All five names were conferred on him when he ascended the throne, even though the last was usually identical with that which he had used before he became king. He could be described as 'the young (or perfect) god' (*netjer nefer*), in comparison to the god Re. His 'divinity' was not the result of an accident of birth, but emanated from his office. It was assumed at his coronation, at which he was accepted as king by the gods of Upper and Lower Egypt; this marked a new beginning, a new 'joining of the Two Lands' and thus a re-enactment of the creation of Egypt after a period of chaos. This cyclical approach to progress and history had its origin in the geographical conditions of the country, with its never-ending regular fluctuation of the river and the change from inundation to the dry season, and the eternal progress of the sun-god through the repeated phases of day and night.

---

* *Papyrus Prisse, 88–9.*

Nevertheless, the Egyptian king was not regarded as another god, but rather as the custodian of the world who secured its smooth functioning. He played an important role which was recognized and acknowledged by the rest of society, and his performance affected everybody. He alone was invested with the authority to intercede with gods on behalf of men. The concept of a powerful and effective intermediary, and an action by proxy, permeates all Egyptian thinking. The Old Kingdom system of provisioning the tombs of *imakhu* is but one reflection of it. The king was thought to make all the offerings and donations to gods in their temples and, in return, to receive a continued approval and support for his rule.

Having been confirmed by gods, the king's supremacy over the world was theoretically absolute. All power and authority were vested in his person, and others could only exercise some of them if these were delegated to them by the king. However, even the king had to rule according to the god-decreed principles of *maet* and his freedom of action was thus restricted. *Maet*, literally 'truth', 'justice', 'righteousness', was a very general concept of 'order' in the world and established relationships in society, and had direct moral implications for each individual. It could be described as a social contract binding for all parties who entered into it in the belief that they would benefit from it. It was the main reason for much of the conservatism which governed Egyptian thinking, and for the reluctance to abandon earlier concepts.

The consequence of the king's position was that he was deemed responsible even for circumstances which were completely beyond his control, such as natural disasters, e.g. a low inundation. The king himself was not thought to have been able to remedy the situation directly, but a natural catastrophe would have been regarded as a failure on his part to perform his duty in maintaining the world's status quo.

The role of the king was, therefore, as much ideological as executive. The dogma concerning his position was proclaimed and re-affirmed by royal rituals, such as coronation and jubilee-festivals (*heb-sed*) while he was alive, and by the building of a monumental pyramidal tomb and the creation of his royal cult establishment for his existence after death. Such material expressions of state ideology soon came to play an essential part in the country's economy, but could only thrive while the premises of Egyptian kingship remained unquestioned. Their demise would have brought down the whole structure of the state.

The king's official dress included a kilt (*shendyt*), the Red (*deshret*) and White (*hedjet*) Crowns, both of different shapes, the crook (*heqat*) and flagellum (*nekhakha*), a ceremonial beard, and a bull's tail attached to the waist.

The king's prime claim to ascend the throne was as his father's son, reflecting the situation of an ordinary family. Ideally, he was the eldest surviving son by the most senior of the queens. There was no automatic right to succeed, and there was no 'divine dynasty' of kings. The blood ties within the royal family can only infrequently be studied in detail and are further complicated because of habitual intermarrying. Unlike their officials and the rest of the population, kings of the Old Kingdom regularly had several consorts, but the term 'harim' which is in general use suggests, wrongly, a large number of concubines. There is, in fact, no evidence for the latter.

Strife and conspiracy may have taken place within the royal family. Thus Weni, an official of the Sixth Dynasty, mentions in a somewhat cryptic fashion in his autobiographical text a trial involving an unnamed queen of Pepy I: 'When the proceedings against the queen, *weret hetes* (a title of queens), were instituted in the royal harim, His Majesty appointed

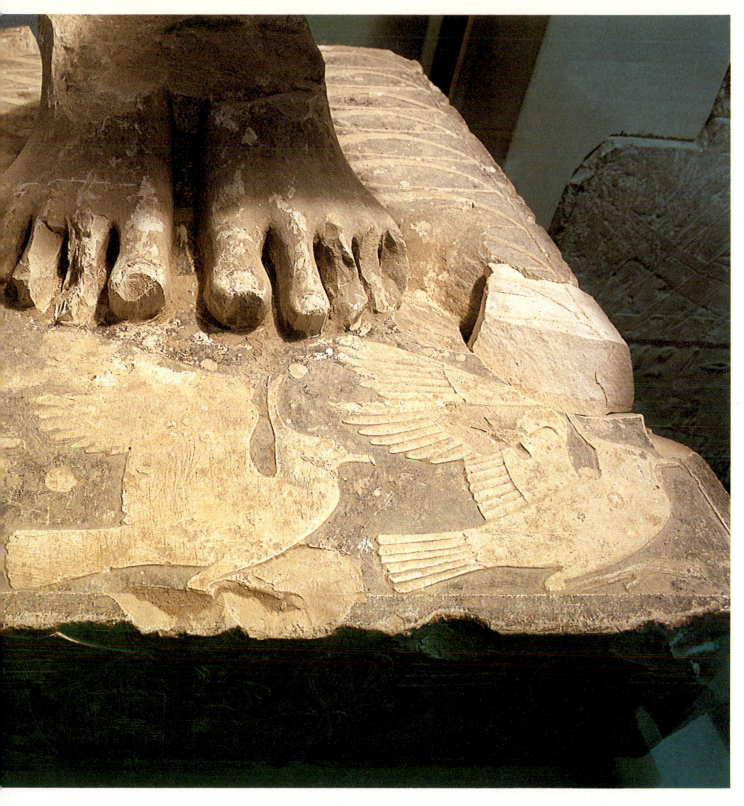

me to hear it privately, with no vizier and chief justice and no official being present except me alone.' The king could choose a queen of non-royal blood, the best-known case being again that of Pepy I who married two daughters, both called Ankh-nes-meryre, of an official Khui from Abdju (Abydos).

The Old Kingdom was a centrally planned and governed bureaucratic state whose theoretical base was the assumption that the king was the guarantor of the existence of the system, but the day-to-day running of the state was in the hands of professional administrators (*seru*, 'officials'). These did not form a special caste but, at least in theory, could be recruited

The feet of King Netjerikhet resting on the 'Nine Bows', representing Egypt's outside enemies, as well as the 'Lapwings' (rekhyt), symbolizing the Egyptian populace, perhaps originally mainly that of the Delta. The king had to dominate both the 'Bows' and the 'Lapwings' in order to fulfil his ideological role in the world. The feet, the base and some fragments are all that remain of this life-size statue.

89

Ipi was a relatively humble 'manager of the estate' (heqa hut). Here he is carried in a palanquin, accompanied by attendants and men with sunshades, on a relief from his Sixth Dynasty tomb at Saqqara.

from any social group. Promotion could be rapid and parvenus may have occasionally posed problems of behaviour, as shown by the following advice from the literary work known as *The Teaching of Ptahhotpe*: 'If you are of humble origin and serve a prominent man, let all your conduct be good before god when you know his former lowly rank. Do not be haughty towards him on account of what you know about his past, but respect him for what has accrued to him, inasmuch as possessions do not come of their own.' Ability and knowledge, but also compliance and

submission, were the best recipe for success and advancement: 'Bend your back to your superior, your overseer of royal administration, then will your house endure in its property, and your rewards will be as they should.' Ethics of the officials of the Old Kingdom were very pragmatic and aimed at ensuring success in this world. They reflected the contemporary understanding of progress, with a return to the same starting point at each new beginning and the maintenance of the status quo. The 'established order' of the Old Kingdom was, according to the prevailing doctrine, perfect and incapable of further improvement, and man's duty was to conform. At the same time, Old Kingdom ethics insisted on correct behaviour and demanded a developed sense of social conscience in the attitude towards the poor and weak.

There are no long genealogies in Old Kingdom tombs displaying the owner's ancestry on which he would have staked a claim to his position in society, and in most cases not even the names of the parents are mentioned. The overall impression is that it was a period of opportunities, when a capable and determined man was appreciated and could make his mark in the world.

The peasants (*meret*) of the Old Kingdom were settled on the land which they cultivated. This could be administered by the state, belong to one of the royal cult or temple establishments, or form part of a tomb endowment. Some of the peasants may even have been attached to privately owned estates. Our information about the details of their legal position is very scanty, but it is clear that they were tied to the land on which they worked and which provided their own living, and had no say in the matter when the land changed hands. They were not free to leave or offer their work elsewhere. At the same time, there is no evidence that they would have been legally regarded as separate items of property and sold as slaves. The Egyptians of the Old Kingdom never really divorced these two elements, the land and its cultivators. It is at least to some extent possible to perceive why. When new farming estates were founded on previously unexploited land, the king had the power to settle them with people from elsewhere. The land presented by him to cult and temple establishments or given as tomb-endowments was already settled, because without people to cultivate it its value would have been limited. On the whole, there was a shortage of labour due to the creation of new estates and the movement of people from farming to other activities. The Egyptian administrative system was so thorough that, almost certainly, all inhabitants were registered so that it was easy to keep check on any population movements. Officials had the use of their 'ex officio' property, but were not allowed to dispose freely of it. This also applied to the personnel settled on the land. Estates of cult and temple establishments and tomb endowments 'belonged' to the deceased kings and officials and to gods, and so they were legally inalienable by the living. The possibilities of transactions involving only people were, therefore, very limited.

War was the only significant source of fresh manpower. We have no precise information on how captives were used and how they were treated. Some were probably settled on the newly recovered land or distributed among existing royal estates, while others may have been employed in quarrying and building. To these people, labour brought by force from abroad, it would be tempting to apply the term 'slaves', though this would be misleading. These prisoners of war did not produce a permanent social group among the Egyptian farming population and did not provide an alternative to the existing method of organization of agricultural production; on the contrary, they were gradually assimilated into the rest of the population.

Craftsmen were attached to institutions, such as the palace or temples. In a royal cult establishment they also doubled as part-time priests. Like the peasants of the establishment with whom they may have shared the 'pyramid-town', they benefited from exemptions granted to their settlement by the king, but unlike them they were in a position to use their free time for private gain. The craftsmen who had to be 'satisfied' in return for work done on private tombs came, no doubt, from royal cult establishments. Their position in society was somewhat ambiguous. They were not their own free agents because they were tied to the cult establishments to which they belonged, but unlike peasants whose surplus produce was probably creamed off most efficiently by their institutions, they were able to accumulate private property.

The only section of Old Kingdom society whose way of life can be reconstructed to some extent is officialdom, including some members of the royal family, because only their tombs contain enough inscriptional and visual evidence concerning daily life. The circumstances of the lives of ordinary peasants and craftsmen are known to us only insofar as they appear as participants in scenes shown in officials' tombs. Their houses have hardly ever been found in excavations. Comparable information concerning the king is completely lacking. The few extant administrative documents deal almost exclusively with affairs of cult establishments, temples, and tomb endowments, and while this information is invaluable for understanding how these institutions worked, it sheds little light on the lives of their ordinary personnel. The texts and decoration of pyramid temples and later the pyramids themselves had matters other than everyday life as their main theme.

Nikanesut was an official of the Fifth Dynasty whose titles suggest that he was in the personal service of the king. He also held several priestly titles, and was a 'king's son of his body', almost certainly an honorific court rank. The closest members of the household of this official are shown in the reliefs of the only decorated room in his tomb-chapel at Giza. Two 'overseers of the property' (*imy-ra per*) called Wehemkai and Kaiemnefert were in overall charge of Nikanesut's estates, though not necessarily simultaneously, and they were supported by eleven 'scribes' (*zesh*). A 'director of the workforce' (*kherep iset*) organized the peasants in the fields, while two 'directors of the dining hall' (*kherep zeh*), two 'overseers of linen' (*imy-ra sesher*), a 'seal-bearer', three butchers, two bakers, one cook, and five butlers looked after the well-being of the tomb-owner at home. Twelve 'servants of the spirit' (*hem-ka*) are shown in the tomb. As in the case of people living in pyramid towns and serving royal cults, 'servants of the spirit' combined ordinary jobs connected with the tomb endowment with part-time assistance at simple ceremonies connected with the maintenance of the funerary cult of the tomb-owner. Another fifteen men of Nikanesut's household represented in his tomb are without an indication of their profession. Other tombs add details to this insight into the organization of an official's property. A 'manager of the estate' (*heqa hut*) was responsible to the 'overseer of the property' for the daily running of each estate, and 'overseers' of 'the stalls' (*imy-ra medjet*) and 'the herds' (*imy-ra tjesut*) for the tomb-owner's cattle. An 'overseer of the storeroom' (*imy-ra per-shena*) supervised the household proper.

Domestic scenes show the tomb-owner at banquets, entertained by music made by flautists and harpists, and by singing and dancing, some of it bordering on acrobatics, or playing the snake (*mehen*) and *senet* board games. His wife—one only, though it seems that there was no specific prohibition regarding polygamy—and his children are often shown

Two circumstances make the identification of this beautifully finished, but uninscribed, greywacke head difficult. Firstly, the number of royal statues of the Old Kingdom unequivocally identified by texts is small, and so for most kings we have few or no comparisons to work with. Secondly, both the White Crown and the Red Crown were worn by gods and goddesses as well as kings, and so the possibility that the head belongs to a statue of a deity cannot be discounted. The sculpture was found near the sun-temple of King Userkaf at Abusir, and probably represents this king. Nevertheless, it is difficult to see in it many similarities with the colossal granite head, also thought to represent Userkaf, from his cult temple at Saqqara.

prominently by his side, accompanied by personal servants and entertainers, some of them dwarfs, and pet dogs and monkeys. Women did not take part in Egyptian administration, but many of those related to officials served as priestesses (*hemet*) of local gods. It seems that legally the position of women in society was not inferior to that of men, and the material well-being of married women was secured by written contracts.

In tomb-scenes, the owner is invariably a dignified, but passive, spectator of activities unfolding in registers before him. Almost the only exceptions are the occasions of hunting fowl in the marshes, where he is standing in a small papyrus raft about to hurl a wooden throw-stick at birds rising out of a papyrus thicket, or fishing, with several fish already impaled on a long barbed spear. These scenes may have soon become a genre rather than a faithful reflection of reality, and so they need not be taken at their full face value, but at the same time their veracity cannot be dismissed completely.

The inauguration of large building projects organized by the state from the beginning of the Third Dynasty led to the creation of a professional administrative system. While previously all high offices were held by the king's relatives, mostly royal princes, commoners now began to be appointed to all but a few positions in administration. Imhotep, the legendary figure reputed to be the architect of Netjerikhet's step pyramid, may have been the first of the eminently capable officials of non-royal blood who now came to the fore.

This development was, no doubt, a consequence of the vast increase in the size of bureaucracy required by the tightly governed centralized state, but it also represented an important change in administration's ideological basis. Royal princes had been able to exercise authority because of their blood relationship to the king, while the power of new officials was delegated to them and was conferred on them through their appointment. A crack separating the executive role of the state and the ideological function of the king and his relatives appeared for the first time in Egyptian history.

The highest Old Kingdom office was that of chief justice and vizier (*taity zab tjaty*) whose control extended over all departments of state administration and the judiciary, and who was directly responsible to the king. The origins of the office are obscure. The votive palette and mace-head of the Predynastic King Narmer show a person described as *tjat*, close to the king, and the etymology of this term is sought in the word (*we*)*tjat*, 'to beget'. Indeed, until the Fifth Dynasty, viziers were exclusively royal princes or their sons. The first vizier known to us by name is Menka, probably of the reign of Netjerikhet, but it was not until the Fourth Dynasty that the office acquired its full status while held by the sons of Kings Snofru, Khufu, Khephren, and Menkaure. When in the Fifth Dynasty even this office passed into the hands of commoners, royal relatives ceased to exert direct influence on the management of state affairs.

The title of vizier underwent a further development first noticeable at the end of the Fifth Dynasty. Some of the titles of Old Kingdom officials were not functional, but conveyed their court rank. The concept probably goes back to the times when the authority to carry out a task on the king's behalf sprang from the official's blood relationship to the king, i.e. his court standing or 'rank'. The importance may not have been purely theoretical and concerned with court protocol, but may have also carried some very practical advantages in the form of benefits to which the holder of such a rank was entitled. Some of the titles which fell in this category soon lost their original meaning and began to be used as rank

indicators. Even the title 'king's son' could be used in this way. Khufu's vizier Hemyunu had the title 'king's son of his body', although it is almost certain that his father was prince Nefermaet. The title of a prince was then conferred on Hemyunu in order to give him the court rank customary for a vizier. By an extension of this idea the title of vizier came to be regarded as a court rank indicator towards the end of the Old Kingdom, and its holders, particularly those who resided in provinces, were not always acting viziers.

An official like a vizier, with his all-embracing powers and complete control, was required because of the extreme fragmentation and complexity of the system of management and the existence of several chains of command. At the same time, individual officials usually concentrated several positions in their hands. This probably enabled them to shortcut procedures and strengthened the overall unity of the system, but it makes it difficult for us to follow how this worked. Officials of state administration were involved in the management of the state treasury, granary, and arsenal, the collection of revenue through taxes and its re-distribution, the imposition of forced labour, the organization of provinces, and various judicial tasks. Many of them played a more immediate economic role in the running of the crown property estates and workshops, or the organization of mining and quarrying expeditions. At the same time, some of them may have held offices connected with the king's household and personal service from which state administration developed in the first place. They may also have been connected in various capacities with royal cult

The concept of the king's right and duty to subjugate foreign lands found early artistic expression on the bases of royal statues which show the heads of prostrate captives. Usually made of a hard stone, in this case granite, these sculptures have been variously dated, but most of them are now attributed to the Third Dynasty. This piece comes from San el-Hagar (Tanis) in the north-eastern Delta, where it had probably been taken for re-use from elsewhere.

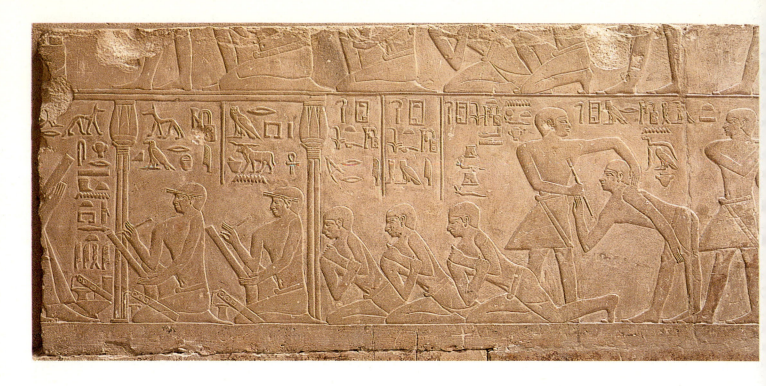

Estate managers (heka hut) *are brought before a council and scribes in order to render accounts of their farms in the early Sixth Dynasty tomb of Mereruka at Saqqara.*

establishments, sun-temples, or temples of local gods. To what extent they were answerable to the vizier in these respects is not clear.

The state treasury, with an overseer (*imy-ra per-hedj*) in charge, collected revenue produced at royal estates and, to a lesser degree, received as taxes. This mostly consisted of various articles of food, but also clothes, tools, furniture, wood, etc., each kept in a special section of the treasury. The storage of grain was administered separately by the state granary (*shenut*), as probably were the arsenal and magazines of oil. The goods kept in these establishments were used to satisfy the requirements of the palace household, but also to pay workmen of the royal workshops. They provided donations in kind presented by the king to pyramid and temple establishments, as well as 'offerings given by the king' to tombs of officials and members of the royal family. All these departments of state administration had large staffs of scribes, and the degree of control over even the smallest transactions must have been considerable. Unfortunately, none of these documents has so far been found.

The idea of justice and administering the law was closely connected with the concept of the world order (*maet*). There were no written laws during the Old Kingdom, but royal decrees issued for institutions as well as to private individuals were recorded and kept in royal archives. The vizier was the supreme judge, and among his titles were 'overseer of the six great courts' (*imy-ra hut-weret issau*), in whose capacity he was in charge of all lawsuits, and 'priest of the goddess Maet' (*hem-netjer maet*). An 'overseer of the great court' (*imy-ra hut-weret*) presumably conducted the legal proceedings, while 'judge and keeper of Nekhen' (*zab iry-nekhen*) was an ancient title of an official who was often involved in special legal proceedings. Only the most important criminal cases were tried in this way. Administration of justice for minor offences, particularly those involving property or dereliction of duty, was probably left in the hands of councils, i.e. the bodies of administrators of each institution. Physical punishment of those found guilty of misdemeanour or negligence, particularly where agricultural production was concerned, was within the confines of a property (*per-djet*) carried out by a body of the 'sons of the property' (*zau-per*).

In the provinces, the organization of royal estates, with the older villages (*niut*) subordinated to them, replaced the loose regional groupings headed by *adj-mer* officials of the first dynasties, which themselves reflected the Predynastic chiefdoms. The district (nome) organization of provinces during the Old Kingdom in which they were gradually transformed is shown almost already fully developed in the reliefs of the valley temple of the southern pyramid of King Snofru at Dahshur. Initially, each district was the responsibility of an 'overseer of commissions' (*imy-ra vepwet*). In the Fifth Dynasty the title of this administrator changed to 'overseer of the district' (*imy-ra*, followed by the hieroglyph of the appropriate district), and in the Sixth Dynasty to 'great overlord of the district' (*hery-tep aa en* + the district sign). The office of an 'overseer of Upper Egypt' (*imy-ra shemau*) with special responsibilities for the southern districts far from the capital, was created in the Fifth Dynasty.

There were twenty-two districts in the valley south of the capital, starting with Ta-sety (present Aswan), while the Delta consisted of fifteen. With the exception of parts of the Delta, particularly the north-eastern and coastal regions, the area administered was much the same as in later times. The provincial capitals of these districts never developed into large urban centres during the Old Kingdom, and their administrative and religious importance far outweighed their size.

Scribes in the Saqqara tomb-chapel of Princess Sesh-seshet Idut of the Sixth Dynasty.

The decoration of the false-door of Nikaure, who was a 'priest [hem-netjer] of the god Re and of the goddess Hathor in the sun-temple of King Neferirkare', displays several unusual features. Relatives are sometimes represented with the tomb-owner, but here Nikaure's mother-in-law Hetepheres and his wife Ihat are shown embracing on the left outer jamb.

There is no evidence of serious social unrest during the Old Kingdom, but we must be aware of the fact that the sources of information at our disposal would probably not reflect them in any case. The Old Kingdom did not know a specialized permanent lawkeeping force or army, though there were some frontier fortresses and garrisons. Their personnel was mostly probably recruited from mercenary Nubians, whose duty was to perform tasks of a small-scale military or police nature. The danger of the military interfering in the affairs of the state was thus non-existent. The approach to any emergency which required a larger military force was the same as in the case of quarrying and mining expeditions. A body of men was conscripted and they were led by their own superiors, with an official appointed by the king in overall charge. The title 'overseer of the task force' (*imy-ra mesha*) applied to the leaders of military as well as peaceful expeditions. Towards the end of the Old Kingdom the same trend appeared as that detectable in trade expeditions, and military enterprises were no longer organized centrally by the state, but were delegated to local officials in border areas.

Throughout the Old Kingdom Egypt enjoyed almost complete safety from foreign intervention, and there was no need for military fortifications within the country. Its superior weapons, but in particular its organization, ensured that nomadic tribes of the deserts on both sides of the Nile soon ceased to present a military threat to its security. Nubia, south of the first Nile cataract, was probably the only area which witnessed vigorous successive campaigns at the beginning of the Old Kingdom, but their motivation was economic and the situation was resolved early in the Fourth Dynasty. Only during the Sixth Dynasty did reports of military actions start to multiply as Egypt's commercial interests and its access to natural resources came under threat, but this never amounted to endangering the existence of the state itself. The only more serious problem which started developing in the north-east during the reign of Pepy I was, apparently, dealt with successfully.

The plunder and the number of captives brought back from expeditions to Nubia in the reign of Snofru are so conspicuously large that they may have been the Egyptians' main motivation. During the early Old Kingdom the Egyptian state embarked on an imperialistic policy of the crudest type directed towards the inhabitants of the Nile valley south of the first cataract. In the Fourth Dynasty an Egyptian settlement existed at Buhen, near the second Nile cataract, but no attempt was made to colonize Nubia or to incorporate it into the general Egyptian administrative system, presumably because of the relatively poor conditions for farming and the shortage of people in Egypt proper. Instead, it was regarded as a source of manpower, cattle, wood, and minerals at the time when Egypt's economy was stretched to the limit because of the monumental building projects. All these resources were exploited to the utmost. The inhabitants of Nubia may have presented problems to Egyptian trade and access to natural resources, but there is nothing to indicate that they would have threatened Egypt's safety at any time. The result was almost complete depopulation of the Nile valley in Nubia, which lasted until the beginning of the Sixth Dynasty, with the inhabitants reduced to migrant nomadic groups.

The situation changed radically in the Sixth Dynasty as the result of population pressures which developed in the south and the abandonment of the previous policy towards Nubia by the Egyptians. The Nubian valley was once again settled. Relations were, at least at first, amicable. Weni, an official of Pepy I, recruited some of the troops for his Asiatic campaign from among 'the Irtjet-Nubians, the Medja-Nubians, the

Yam–Nubians, the Wawat–Nubians, and the Kaau–Nubians'. A rock inscription in the Aswan area records that King Merenre in person received Nubian chiefs there in the 'year of the fifth census', during which 'the chiefs of Medja, Irtjet, and Wawat were kissing the ground and were giving very great adoration'. Weni was actively helped by the Nubians during the same reign: 'His Majesty sent me to excavate five canals in Upper Egypt and to build three barges and four boats of acacia of Wawat, while the chiefs of Irtjet, Wawat, Yam, and Medja provided wood for them. I achieved it all in a single year.' Relations deteriorated towards the end of the Sixth Dynasty: Egypt's might was on the decline, while the power of Nubian chiefs was ascendant. Armed clashes and retributive expeditions led by administrators of the southernmost district of Egypt were frequently reported.

Two women playing the harp and singing are represented in another small scene on Nikaure's false-door. Although dating to the first half of the Fifth Dynasty, the false-door adopted some of the themes of decoration of the chapels, and so anticipated trends more common towards the end of the Old Kingdom.

Children playing games, from the early Sixth Dynasty tomb of Mereruka at Saqqara.

Facing page: The vizier Ptahhotpe carried in a palanquin, on the left outer jamb of the stela (false-door) in his tomb at Saqqara.

Although the record of an enormous Libyan booty accompanies a relief in the pyramid temple of Sahure at Abusir, its value as historical evidence is in doubt. With some exceptions in the Fourth Dynasty, military actions against the tribes living to the west of the Nile valley must have been very limited. The reason for this lack of interest on the parts of the Egyptians was that this region possessed a relatively small economic importance.

Egypt's relations with the areas to the east and north-east were of a more aggressive nature, aimed at securing access to the resources of the Sinai. Clashes with the nomads inhabiting the Eastern Desert and Sinai are listed on the Palermo Stone, and their subjugation symbolically proclaimed in rock inscriptions at Sinai.

Large-scale campaigning took place in Palestine during the reign of Pepy I and was described in the autobiographical text of Weni: 'His Majesty sent me to lead this army five times in order to destroy the land of the sand-dwellers every time they rebelled, with these troops.' It seems that the preventive measures taken by the Egyptians were caused by security considerations of a more serious nature, because they required a large number of troops. In two private tombs of the Sixth Dynasty, those of Kaemhest at Saqqara and of Inti at Dishasha, there are representations of a siege of a fortified town which may reflect these campaigns. For the first time in Egyptian military history we even get a glimpse of tactics employed in the engagement against desert raiders. Weni describes it as follows: 'I crossed in boats with these troops and landed behind a hill of a ridge to the north of the land of the sand-dwellers, while half of this army of mine was on the road. I came, captured all of them, and killed every raider among them.'

SEVEN

GODS AND TOMBS

'Look up, you gods who are in the netherworld! King Unas has come, having become the great god, so that you may see him.' ★

King Unas suckled by an unknown goddess, on a relief from his cult temple at Saqqara. In most cases, the decoration of the cult temples is known to us only from isolated and very incomplete scenes. The temples, which have yielded more substantial areas of the original decorated surface, are those of Sahure at Abusir, and of Pepy II at Saqqara, but even they are in a very dilapidated state.

EACH SECTION OF THE EGYPTIAN POPULATION had its own ideas and beliefs, representing attempts to come to terms with the forces of nature and society beyond man's understanding. The official dogma concerning the king, reflected in the reliefs of the royal pyramid-complexes and the texts inscribed inside the pyramids, had little in common with the spiritual life of the majority of the Egyptian population and would have been scarcely comprehensible to them. The relationship of the individual to the state, embodied in the king, or to the local gods, as well as ideas about continued existence after death, affected the life of everyone, but to varying degrees. In Egypt different aspects of spiritual life were inextricably fused into one. Although we use terms such as 'religion', 'ideas about life after death', and 'state doctrine', to try to disentangle them is impossible. These ideas developed historically and were subjected to much re-interpretation, and did not form a perfect system without contradictions. The overall picture of the situation during the Old Kingdom presented to us by the available sources is very incomplete and unbalanced, and we are to some extent dependent on assumptions drawn from later times.

The belief in a local god, connected with a particular area and with limited powers, and local myths, was at the root of Old Kingdom religion. The Egyptian pantheon was thus a complicated system of deities of varying nature and significance, with little resembling a strict hierarchical order. Different gods originally played similar roles in various parts of the country, and there were varying approaches to the concepts of creation and cosmology. With the appearance of a unified state came attempts in the main religious centres, such as Iunu (Heliopolis) and Ineb-hedj (Memphis), to rationalize this situation, but they never developed further during the Old Kingdom, and the precise stages of this process are not clear.

The importance of the gods and their mutual relationship changed as did their local areas. Some of the local deities were recognized and accepted, even outside their home districts, by the top intellectual section of Egyptian society, but they almost certainly played no part in the spiritual life of humbler people. It was only the local god, and perhaps a few other deities associated with him, who was really significant for an ordinary individual whose religious outlook remained confined to the area where he lived. In the case of officials, the reasons for this limited outlook could be of a more materialistic nature, such as serving as a priest in the local god's traditional temple. It is likely that the peasant population

---

★ *Pyramid Texts, §272.*

also worshipped a host of minor deities about whom we know little because of their 'semi-official' nature. These found little reflection on monuments which are rarely associated with the lowest stratum of Egyptian society. Our awareness of them is based on material of later periods.

Nearly every god of the earliest part of Egyptian history was visualized in the form of an animal, bird, or even an inanimate object. Thus Bastet, the local goddess of the town Bast (modern Tell Basta) in the eastern Delta, became associated with a lioness, the god Thoth of Khemenu (Hermopolis Magna, modern El-Ashmunein) with an ibis, Khnum of the first cataract region with a ram, the goddess Hathor, whose worship was known from several places, with a cow, and the god Sobek with a crocodile. The precise reasons for such associations are not clear, but natural logic seems to have influenced the choice. Thus, the cults of the bull were popular in the cattle-grazing area of the Delta, a crocodile cult was known from the marshy Faiyum, etc. The god could adopt the form of an animal in order to become manifest, but this did not mean the animal itself was regarded as a deity. An unsophisticated mind prefers to think in terms of visual images rather than abstract concepts, and the system of local deities reflects the earliest stages of the development of Egyptian religious thought.

Attempts to endow gods, in particular the ancient god Min of Gebtiu (Koptos, modern Qift) and Ptah of Ineb-hedj (Memphis), with human forms date to the end of the Predynastic Period or shortly afterwards. This may have been due to their relatively late rise to prominence, or to the need to devise a more accessible image for these deities. So the ithyphallic god Min, one of the most ancient and most important local gods of the Old Kingdom, had previously been worshipped as a curious harpoon-like object (fetish), the precise nature of which is not clear. And when the capital moved to the north, the god Ptah benefited greatly from his connection with the area and became the most prominent among local gods of the Old Kingdom. The image of a deity represented with human characteristics shows a completely different understanding of the nature of gods because previously the contrast between man and the forces of nature was the very basis of primitive religion.

A combination of human and animal features in one form, e.g. the representation of the goddess Bastet as a woman with the head of a lioness, was a typically Egyptian artistic device, rather than a religious development in its own right. It became the usual form in which the deity appeared in official reliefs and statues, but did not contain additional significance. For most people, to whom official temples were closed, the fully zoomorphic idea of their local god remained the deity's main manifestation.

Two gods, originally connected with particular localities and thus local deities, became closely associated with the concept of kingship and the person of the king, and acquired special status. Horus and Seth were the two most influential gods of the earliest part of Egyptian history, the former represented as a hawk (*heru* means 'one who is distant' or 'one who is high'), the latter as an obscure animal which at first resembled a donkey. They were the local gods of the Upper Egyptian towns Nekhen and Nubt, and their connection with the early kings thus had a historical justification. It seems, however, that by the time the religious significance of these towns became reflected in the court art of the late Predynastic Period their former political importance was already a thing of the past. The unique position of these gods in no way implied a popular worship.

Most of the local gods, recognized by the state and regarded as representatives of their home districts, are attested from the earliest dynasties. Because of the role the king played in the world he alone could, as an intermediary, communicate with gods on behalf of men. This meant that monuments directly reflecting the attitudes of officials and still humbler people to these gods are practically non-existent during the Old Kingdom. Our information derives mostly from such meagre sources as personal names (e.g. the common name Ptahhotpe can be translated as 'The God Ptah is Satisfied', Nefer-her-sokar as 'The Face of the God Sokar is Beautiful', and Ankh-hathor as 'May the Goddess Hathor Live!'), the priesthoods held by tomb-owners and their relatives, the names of their estates recorded in tombs, and the names of gods listed in offering-texts on stelae and elsewhere in tombs. At his coronation, the king had to secure approval from local gods for his reign, and in addition to being responsible for the welfare of men on earth and in the afterlife, he was expected to maintain the shrines of local gods and to provide offerings for them and provisions for the upkeep of their priesthood.

This 'official' popular religion of the Old Kingdom, supported by the king, was very much based on the carrying out of rituals. The shrines were served by semi-professional 'servants of the god' (*hem-netjer*), recruited from local officials. The buildings, with their mud-brick walls and no relief decoration, were modest affairs, and this explains why so little of them has survived. They were situated in towns, not in the desert like royal cult temples and sun-temples, and thus fell victim to later alterations and re-building. The making of cult-statues for these sanctuaries is recorded in the 'annals', but hardly any have survived. This may be due to the fact that often their material, such as metal or wood, was re-used in later times. It is likely that the daily ritual in these temples was

For most people, it is the pyramids which symbolize the achievements of the Old Kingdom civilization. Their silent massive structures inspire awe and wonder, but standing before them we hardly feel that we are in direct contact with the thought and work of living people of a bygone age. The reconstructed wooden barque, originally found dismantled in a 'boat-pit' near the south-eastern corner of Khufu's pyramid, has the power to produce such an effect. Thousands of years of religion, mastery over the material, and nautical skill, are contained in this beautiful craft. Almost all the materials used in the boat's reconstruction are ancient. The shape is that of a sacred barque (wia), with a tall prow and stern, and the boat was probably used during Khufu's funeral. Yet another boat may still rest in a similar pit further to the west.

quite simple and consisted of taking the image of the god out of its shrine, cleansing, clothing, and anointing it, and offering it symbolic food and drink. Religious festivals were celebrated, and it was probably only on these occasions that ordinary people, who otherwise did not have access to the temple, had a chance to see the image of the local god.

At first, the main beneficiaries of the king's favours were the religious centres near the capital, and it appears that it was only in the Fifth Dynasty that temples even in the provinces began to receive land donations which turned them into economically independent institutions. It is possible that this was at first little more than a convenient substitute for the previous method of provisioning, but it proved of great importance for the growing economic self-reliance of the officials who were attached to these temples in priestly capacities. The king's greater interest in the shrines of local gods could have been the consequence of an earlier development. It seems that the official dogma concerning the king's relationship with the gods was re-defined and systematized during the Fourth Dynasty in order to make him part of a system with the creator sun-god Re (or, in a syncretized form, Re-Harakhti, 'Re-Horus of the Horizon') of Iunu

'Boat-pits' are often situated near Old Kingdom pyramids. They are of two types: those which imitate the shape of ceremonial barques, as e.g. the 'boat-pit' near the south-eastern corner of Radjedef's pyramid at Abu Rawash, and the rectangular pits which contain dismantled wooden boats. The stone replicas of barques are presumably connected with the idea of sky voyages on which the king was to accompany the sun-god. There can be several such boats round a cult temple and pyramid.

Scenes showing Meryre-nufer Qar's funeral in his Sixth Dynasty tomb at Giza. In the upper register, a lector-priest, an embalmer, and a professional female mourner lead the cortège to the purification-house. In the register below, the coffin is transported in a boat to the embalming-house.

(Heliopolis) at the head. The rise in importance of the sun-god led to his recognition as the main state-god of the Old Kingdom, and the appearance of the name of the god in royal names and titles reflected it. The king, while still being called Horus, now became a 'son of the god Re'.

The first three kings of the Fifth Dynasty, according to a later popular tradition, originated in the union of the sun-god and the wife of a priest of Re. A series of sun-temples was built for the god's worship. From Userkaf to Menkauhor—except for the ephemeral Shepseskare—each king made a new sun-temple on a fresh site near the capital and not far away from his pyramid. This was a concept entirely different from the building or enlargement of temples of local gods on traditional locations, and was unique to the Fifth Dynasty. It was clearly regarded as each king's duty during his reign. The god Re as the chief state god was treated in the same way as the king, his representative on earth. The king built a pyramid and a cult establishment for himself, and a sun-temple for the worship of the state god where he stressed the god's relationship to his own reign. These temples received large donations of offerings and land, had their own personnel, and for much of the Fifth Dynasty were the most important economic institutions in the country after the state.

The increased influence of pyramid establishments in the second half of the Fifth Dynasty followed the decline and cessation of the building of sun-temples. The reasons behind this decline were very likely purely economic, rather than ideological, the system no longer being able to sustain the demanding construction schedule of both projects and the endowing of both institutions during a single reign.

Apart from the local god one other deity with local connections figured very prominently in the thoughts of the Egyptians of the Old Kingdom. It was the god of the local necropolis, such as Khentiamentiu at Abdju (Abydos) and Sokar in the Ineb-hedj (Memphis) region, and universally Anubis, usually associated with the jackal, and later Osiris. At a man's death one of the elements of his personality, 'vital force' or 'spirit' (ka), continued to exist in the tomb, while the deceased himself became an akh-spirit after the accomplishment of the prescribed funeral rites. The body was deemed necessary for the ka's continued existence, and attempts to provide a substitute abode for it led to the introduction of tomb statues. The same belief prompted the first experiments with artificial preservation (mummification). The ka's material needs were similar to those of

Like the exterior of early brick-built mastabas, painted decoration of uninscribed false-doors of the Old Kingdom sometimes imitated mat patterns. The tomb of Ptahhotpe at Saqqara, shown here, dates from the end of the Fifth Dynasty.

The chapel (i.e. the part of the tomb which was above ground and accessible) of a large mastaba of the Fifth or Sixth Dynasty could consist of a number of porticos, corridors, halls, courts, store-rooms, etc. The most important among them was the offering-room with a false-door. Unusually, in the mastaba of Mereruka the pillared hall contains a niche with an offering-table and a statue of the tomb-owner.

the living, and food and drink offerings were brought to the tomb's chapel which was the only part publicly accessible. In the absence of real offerings, these could be provided symbolically by representations on the stela (false-door) or tomb walls, or by recitation of prescribed formulae. The activities represented in Old Kingdom tombs which are connected with such provisioning are thus meant to be taking place very much in this world, not in any version of an Egyptian paradise.

The god of the necropolis was regarded as the ruler of the dead buried in his area. The provisioning of officials' tombs was originally seen as a transaction involving the king as the donor, the necropolis-god as the main beneficiary, and the tomb-owner as a participant allowed to share some of the offerings with the necropolis-god. No gods except those connected with the necropolis played any part in the ideas concerning afterlife reflected in private tombs of the Old Kingdom, and scenes involving gods were never shown in them. The strict division between the king and ordinary men in this world was thus continued in the arrangements made for the afterlife.

While ordinary spirits continued to exist in the realm of the god of the local necropolis, the king was originally thought to depart after his death to the polar star in the sky, the celestial region of the goddess Nut, and the abode of gods whom he joined there. He could adopt various forms and use various means to reach the sky, where he accompanied the sun-god in his barque in order to traverse the sky with him. The beliefs concerning this form of afterlife, probably closely related to the sky and solar concepts of Iunu (Heliopolis), are known to us from the Pyramid Texts. These were the texts inscribed inside the pyramids of kings and several queens from the end of the Fifth Dynasty. The Pyramid Texts contain religious and funerary spells and parts of myths of various dates and thus represent a mixture of widely differing concepts. They were probably included in an attempt to ensure that the king had them to hand if knowledge of them was required in his existence after death. Some of these texts may have been recited during the ceremonies accompanying the funeral.

The dead king is, however, in the Pyramid Texts also identified with the god Osiris. Osiris was originally a chthonic deity. At first, he perhaps assimilated the god Anedjti, and became connected with the town of Djedu (Busiris) in the central Delta, and very early on also Iunu (Heliopolis). His importance grew rapidly, and he may have, as early as the Fourth Dynasty, influenced the changes in the royal pyramid-complexes. In private tombs Osiris began to be mentioned in the Fifth Dynasty, which is also the earliest date at which he was represented in human form. He quickly acquired the status of the universal god of the nether-world, with Djedu (Busiris) and Abdju (Abydos) as his main cult centres. In Abdju, he assimilated the original god Khentiamentiu. Throughout the Old Kingdom only the king was identified after death with the god Osiris.

Much of the mythology known to us from later periods of Egyptian history must have already existed during the Old Kingdom. The myth of Seth's killing his brother Osiris, of the goddesses Isis and Nephthys' mourning over his body, and his eventual vindication by Horus, is already suggested in the Pyramid Texts.

Although a vast body of material is available for the student of religion during the later periods of Egyptian history, information concerning the Old Kingdom is very limited. No papyri with religious texts have been found, and only afterlife aspects are stressed in private tombs. Royal pyramid-complexes are almost the only source of reliefs showing gods, and the Pyramid Texts represent the only large corpus of inscriptions. Temples of local gods are virtually unknown.

In private tombs, the west-oriented stela (false-door) was thought to be a link connecting the world of the living and the world of the dead. The ka of the tomb-owner partook of the offerings of food and drink brought to the false-door which was the focal point of the tomb-chapel. The false-door invariably carried several representations of the tomb-owner in relief, but exceptionally one or more of these were made three-dimensional, probably influenced by statues which became an integral part of rock-cut tombs. This figure of Idu, half-emerging from the ground in his Sixth Dynasty tomb at Giza, strikes us as rather absurd in its concept, but it is interesting both for the imagery which inspired it, and because it demonstrates the close relationship between 'two-dimensional' reliefs and three-dimensional statues.

EIGHT

TOMB-ARTISTS AND THE WORLD

'The draughtsman of the temple of the goddess Matit, Pepy-sonb, whose real name is Nesu.' ★

All statues of the Old Kingdom were functional, i.e. made to play a particular role in a temple, pyramid-complex, or tomb. With a few exceptions, art for art's sake did not exist, and artistic development was thus nothing but the search for a better way of fulfilling the sculpture's formal role or, at best, working within tightly prescribed limits. Sometimes statues were part of the decorative programme of a temple or a tomb. At other times they were regarded as an embodiment of the physical characteristics of the king or the tomb-owner, in order to provide an abode for the spirit (ka) if anything should happen to the corpse. The statues of Prince Rahotpe shown on page 113 and his wife Nofret pictured here come from their early Fourth Dynasty tomb at Maidum. Although made separately, they were intended as a pair.

SINCE MUCH OF OUR KNOWLEDGE of everyday life in Egypt during the Old Kingdom derives from reliefs in tomb-chapels, an understanding of the conventions of tomb art of this period and an appreciation of the limits of the artist's creative freedom are essential for interpreting this evidence.

The Egyptian canon, or fixed system of proportions according to which the human body was represented, appeared in a rudimentary form in late Predynastic court art. The same was true of the conventional way in which the body was seen: face and mouth in profile, eye and eyebrow in full view, chest and shoulders in front view, but waist and legs again in profile. The picture of the human figure is thus a composite view which could never be seen by one pair of eyes at one time. The Egyptian artist, however, sought a compromise in this approach to the portrayal of reality, and while he adhered to the concept that all essential parts must be represented and shown in their most characteristic views, he assembled these elements in a way which was as close as possible to how he normally saw them as a whole. Sometimes even such paradoxical combinations as joining the left arm to the right shoulder and vice versa seemed a small price to pay in order to reconcile the two contradictory methods. This prescribed way of showing human figures applied rigorously to the protagonists in tomb scenes, but to a lesser degree to the representations of minor participants. The greatest freedom of expression the artist enjoyed was in the portrayal of animals.

The same 'mosaic' approach can be seen in the composition of large scenes. The relative heights of figures were important inasmuch as they helped to distinguish between protagonists and participants, and since the whole scene was approached through its individual elements, the difference in sizes was not felt to disturb the balance of the composition. A large seated figure of a man may be accompanied by a diminutive representation of his wife squatting by his legs, or the tomb-owner may be shown absurdly large in comparison with the small figures of his sons.

Egyptian art did not develop a concept of perspective similar to ours, although some points of agreement may be found. Distances from the viewer were indicated by the relative positions of partly overlapping representations along the horizontal rather than the vertical axis, but these remained on the same base-line. In a large composition the area was

★ *Artist's signature alongside the staff held by the official Djau in his late Sixth Dynasty tomb at Deir el-Gebrawi.*

divided into several horizontal registers delineated by such base-lines. The orientation of the scenes within each register was determined by the large figure in the composition, e.g. if the scene was one of 'inspection' carried out by the tomb-owner, the smaller figures in the registers were bringing the inspected goods or animals towards him. In the absence of a protagonist who could serve as a focal point, the orientation was subordinated to the tomb's architecture, e.g. the false-door stela, to which the scenes were oriented.

Symmetry and inner logic also played an important part. Large representations of the tomb-owner on door-jambs are always symmetrically arranged, and the logic manifests itself by the tomb-owner always coming out of his tomb to 'meet' the visitor. In pillared halls, with representations of the deceased often occupying all four faces of the pillars, the route the visitor is to take is virtually signposted in this way.

Actions, or a continuous series of occurrences, were recorded by a selection of typical situations or phases. The lowest register on the wall usually contained the most recent episodes or those concluding the cycle. This arrangement, albeit operating along the temporal rather than spatial axis, is to some extent comparable to our notion of perspective.

The themes into which the decoration is divided do not always correspond to individual walls of the tomb-chapel, and corners of rooms thus do not necessarily represent dividing lines. Certain walls became associated with specific subjects, but because of the great diversity of the plans of chapels only very general rules developed. Texts which accompany the scenes may describe the action represented, record the conversation of the participants, or give their names and those of the objects shown, but in many cases they only serve as a convenient way of filling space. Large empty areas were regarded as failings on the part of the designer and sculptor.

The designer of the decoration of a tomb-chapel was thus subjected to restrictions of several types. The proportions and the way figures were portrayed were firmly established, as were the general principles of the spatial distribution of scenes on the wall. The main themes of decoration were more or less obligatory, and also their position in the chapel was indicated if not prescribed. The techniques and the choice of colours were in most respects the same in all tombs. All this was the consequence of the very pragmatic function of tomb decoration in securing the tomb-owner's afterlife. The designer was not allowed to put this at risk by giving a free rein to his artistic inclinations or by experimenting. His task was to execute the required design which had proved its effectiveness in the past. Yet there are no two tomb-chapels with identical decoration, and the number of wall-scenes which are similar to the point of identity could be counted on the fingers of one hand. This shows beyond any doubt that the artist had some freedom to create, and that this freedom was consciously sought, the opportunities seized, and new solutions to old problems perhaps even demanded by those who paid for the work.

Each theme which appears in the decoration of Old Kingdom chapels can be broken up into a number of smaller episodes. Thus the agricultural theme may include ploughing, sowing, treading the grain, reaping, filling sacks with sheaves, bringing a donkey-herd, loading donkeys, transport of grain to threshing floors, threshing, winnowing, and storing grain in granaries, to mention just the more common topics. The first freedom of choice the artist was able to exercise was in the matter of composition. As a rule, more than just one theme appeared on the same wall, and the artist was able to decide how he was going to divide the

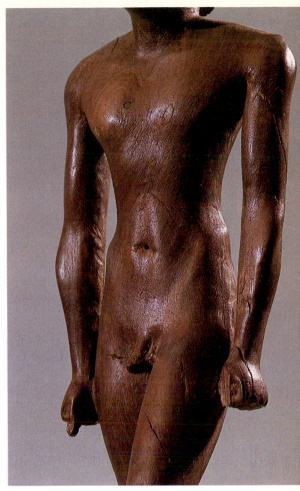

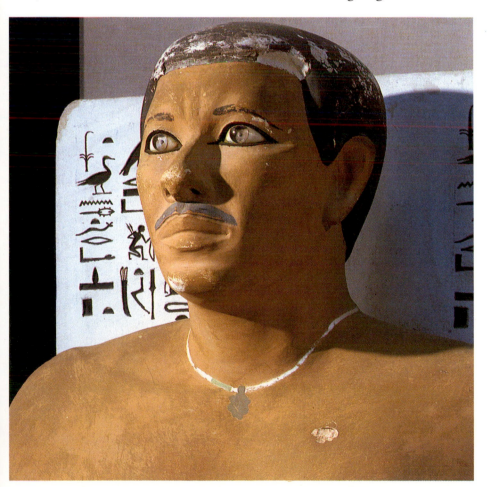

Above: The materials of private statues varied as much as those of royal sculptures, but the majority of them were made of the most accessible, limestone and wood. In the stone statues of the Old Kingdom it is still possible to discern the influence of the shape of the original block of material, but some wooden statues were now freed of the rigidity of the block: arms and hands were no longer attached to the body, and the sceptre and the staff were held in the hands in a natural way, not pressed against the torso. The material thus exercised a considerable influence over the development of form. This Sixth Dynasty statue of Meryre-haishtef was, unusually, carved of a single piece of ebony wood, and comes from Sidmant in Middle Egypt.

Left: A statue's uniqueness was guaranteed by its inscription. The text above the right shoulder of Rahotpe's statue is arranged in three vertical columns (hieroglyphs could be written horizontally as well as vertically), and describes him as 'overseer of the task force', 'director of bowmen', and 'King's son of his body'. The last five signs at the bottom of the left column record his name.

*The 'overseer of sculptors'
Niankhptah left a portrait of himself in the
chapel of Ptahhotpe at Saqqara, whose reliefs
he may have carved.*

available space among them. Secondly, he had to select the episodes of each of the themes to be included. Thirdly, he chose how they were going to be shown. Even the most banal episodes, such as in the scenes of butchery, occur in countless varieties. The artist may have learnt to treat a particular episode in a number of different ways during his training, or he may have had patterns at his disposal from which he copied on the wall. The most attractive and probably the likeliest idea is that during his apprenticeship he had learnt to draw detailed elements of these episodes. A hand could be shown as holding a butcher's knife, or a flint knife-sharpener, or a leg of the slaughtered animal. A bent figure of a butcher might be completed to show him cutting off a leg of the slaughtered animal or extracting the heart. An upright figure could be supplied with various cuts of meat to carry. The artist's freedom thus in most cases consisted of being able to choose and combine prescribed elements of scenes in his own individual way to achieve the expected overall effect. Sometimes the artist's originality may have shown itself in an entirely new feature of his own added to the existing repertoire, and this was then adopted by others and became a standard element, while outdated and no longer fashionable scenes may have been abandoned. The distinction between a craftsman faithfully following a well-trodden path and a creative artist was very fine indeed, and often blurred.

Men responsible for the design and carving of tomb reliefs and statues were regarded in the same way as those who built the tomb or made its funerary equipment. The work on the construction of a tomb is never represented, but sculptors carving statues are often shown next to men making stone vessels, as well as carpenters and other craftsmen. In most cases they remained completely anonymous. Inscriptions in the Fourth Dynasty tomb of Nebemakhet at Giza, accompanying representations of two men, state that 'it was the painter Semerka, one rewarded by him (i.e. by the tomb-owner), who made his tomb', and 'it was Inkaf, one rewarded by him, who executed the work on his tomb'. They are very exceptional. A more common ploy was to introduce the figures of the artists among the small representations of offering-bearers. The most flagrant of such cases perhaps is that of the sculptor who was responsible for the magnificent reliefs in the Fifth Dynasty tomb of Ptahhotpe at Saqqara. On the north wall of the chapel, next to the scene of three papyrus rafts with boatmen engaged in a mock battle, is a small skiff showing the 'overseer of sculptors' Niankh-ptah well supplied with food and helping himself freely from a large jar of beer offered to him by a small boy. This artist, at least, seemed to have been quite content with his inconspicuous lot.

Statues formed a very important feature of private tombs, and scenes showing them dragged on sleds to the tombs are not uncommon in reliefs. Pictured here is a Sixth Dynasty mastaba of Princess Sesh-seshet Idut at Saqqara.

NINE

THE COLLAPSE

'Indeed, the ship of the southerners has gone adrift; towns are destroyed and Upper Egypt has become empty wastes.'★

WHEN PEPY II ASCENDED THE THRONE AT the age of six in 2247 BC, Egypt had been suffering from deep-rooted inner weaknesses for some time. Nevertheless, the tremendous momentum acquired during the uninterrupted progress from the beginning of the Predynastic Period carried the country onward until the compounded effects of the general malaise ripped apart the fabric of its society at the end of the Sixth Dynasty. The full impact of this became apparent during the First Intermediate Period.

The looming threat materialized shortly after Pepy II's immensely long rule of over ninety years. The strife for his succession created a political crisis which was reflected in the very short reign of one year and one month of one of his many sons, Merenre-Nemtyemzaf. It was followed by the probably unprecedented installation of a woman, Queen Neitiqert, on the Egyptian throne. The next seventeen rulers of the Seventh and Eighth Dynasties of Manetho shared only some sixteen years between them. Confusion must have permeated the whole system, until eventually the country came to be split into two large areas controlled by the rulers from Henen-nesut (Herakleopolis, modern Ihnasya el-Medina) and Waset (Thebes, modern Luxor).

Monumental building slowly ground to an almost complete halt. The pyramid of Pepy II was the last really large undertaking of the Old Kingdom. Only one of the pyramids of the following years has been located at Saqqara, and its reduced size and very simple construction are a telling illustration of the diminished royal power. Private tombs built near the capital from the mid-Sixth Dynasty onward became smaller and their decoration was frequently restricted to their painted burial chambers, and thus reflected a comparable trend in the declining prosperity of officialdom.

The body of Ankh-nes-pepy, a minor queen of Pepy II and the mother

A profound knowledge of history or architecture is not necessary in order to date Old Kingdom pyramids. It is enough to look at their present silhouettes: the step pyramid of Netjerikhet is of the Third Dynasty, while the pyramids proper which present a clean and sharp outline against the sky date from the Fourth Dynasty; those of the Fifth and Sixth Dynasties are now ragged shapes resembling huge piles of stone blocks and rubble. Less careful work, in particular the use of smaller blocks, is the reason for this decline. In this view of northern Saqqara, the pyramids, from the left, belong to Netjerikhet, Userkaf, and Teti.

★ *Papyrus Leiden 344 recto, 2,11.*

of one of his successors, was found buried in a re-used sarcophagus, a sad comment on the conditions which affected even the highest-ranking members of the royal family at this time. The last dated inscription at Wadi Maghara in the Sinai is of Pepy II's second census, probably his third year. The lack of later inscriptions was due to the government's reduced ability to finance large-scale mining expeditions and to the fall in demand for exclusive materials. Also the dangers of attack by hostile tribesmen seem to have increased dramatically, at least partly because the policing of border areas was less assiduously pursued. Pepynakht Heqaib describes in his tomb how he was sent to the country of the Aamu in order to bring back the body of an official 'building a ship there for a journey to Punt when the Aamu of the sand-dwellers killed him together with the troops who were with him'. The situation was particularly serious in Nubia and required measures reminiscent of the drastic military actions at the beginning of the Old Kingdom. The same Pepynakht describes one of these raids: 'The Majesty of my lord sent me to hack up the countries of Wawat and Irtjet. I did as my lord praises. I killed there a large number, including chief's children and commanders of élite troops. I brought a large number from there to the Residence as captives while I was at the head of a large and mighty army as a hero.'

Climatic conditions started worsening around the beginning of the Sixth Dynasty, and the disastrous consequences of this, particularly of the lower level of Nile inundations, became fully apparent when the central government disintegrated. Many texts of the period which followed the end of the Old Kingdom describe the famine which raged through the land. Ankh-tifi, the 'great overlord of the districts of Edfu and Hierakonpolis' during the Seventh or Eighth Dynasty, describes the desperate situation which developed in the south: 'Upper Egypt in its entirety was dying of hunger, everybody eating his children, but I never allowed it to happen that anyone died of hunger in this district.'

The conditions which existed in parts of Egypt during this unhappy period may have served as inspiration for two later literary works, the *Admonitions of Ipuwer*, and the *Prophecies of Neferti*. Both of them were composed for propagandist reasons, and the desperate situation provided them with a contrast for the happier times to come. Because of this, it is sometimes difficult to accept their vivid imagery as a faithful reflection of reality. It is also their poetic language which makes them remarkable. 'A man goes out to plough with his shield.' 'Indeed, many dead are buried in the river. The stream is a tomb, and the place of embalmment has become a stream.' 'Indeed, laughter has perished, and is no longer made, and it is grief which is throughout the land, mixed with lamentation.' 'Behold, he who was ignorant of the lyre now owns a harp.'

There are many factors to be taken into account when we look for the causes of Egypt's sudden decline during this period. The Egyptian state of the Old Kingdom was created and existed because of certain ideological preconditions which had their roots in the preceding periods. State and religious ideology, fused into one, had to be maintained by material means if the state was to survive with its basic characteristics intact. This entailed the monumental building of pyramids for the deceased kings and, even more important, the endowment of their cult establishments. Similar provisions, though on a much smaller scale, had to be made for the rest of the ruling hierarchy. Gigantic building enterprises used up huge amounts of contemporary resources and, no doubt, created economic strains. Such use of resources, however, was ideologically essential, and to direct the effort differently, towards more productive objectives, e.g. irrigation, was not an option which was really available in the framework

of the existing society. The endowment of royal cult establishments in itself did not represent a material loss because the surplus was re-distributed in various ingenious ways to filter through to larger sections of society. If certain practical difficulties could be overcome, it is conceivable to envisage a society whose total national product is first applied to satisfying the needs of the dead, and then used to sustain the living.

Nor can it be said that the growing power of temples, resulting from endowments and exemptions of their properties from state obligations, caused any losses in real terms. The Egyptian method of 'offering' to deities did not involve extensive waste of material and the numbers of the professional priesthood were very small.

The Old Kingdom was not brought to its knees by an upheaval caused by a popular uprising. The graphic descriptions of Ipuwer and Neferti depict chaotic conditions during a period of social instability, but hardly an attempt by the exploited class to change the social system. For the majority of the Egyptian population the question of the ownership of the land on which they worked was of limited consequence. Even such things as exemption from state duties and forced participation in state enterprises were of more concern to the landowner than to the peasants.

No large-scale invasion of the country from abroad took place at the end of the Old Kingdom. The increased insecurity in border areas, due

The fertile soil under cultivation can change into the barren sand of the desert virtually in a few yards. These were the most sensitive areas of the Black Land (Kemet) where even temporary neglect or lack of water had an immediate effect. The valley temples and the pyramids at Abusir could, to all appearances, be located in two different worlds.

119

Facing page: The starving people on this relief, almost certainly from the causeway of Unas at Saqqara, are not necessarily inhabitants of the Nile valley. Similar scenes, however, must have become commonplace even in Egypt, particularly in the south, at the end of the Old Kingdom.

The Great Pyramid seen through the crumbling superstructure of the Old Kingdom Mastabas.

to the failure of the weak administration to police them, at no point escalated into a decisive attack. The situation in Nubia was caused by climatic and ethnic pressures outside Egypt's sphere of influence, but it is likely that a strong government would have been able to safeguard its interests even there.

Egypt had had problems with royal succession even earlier, e.g. in the second half of the Fourth Dynasty, but these were always overcome and left no permanent scars on its society. The long reign of Pepy II, which in its last years probably was rather ineffectual, must have aggravated the situation, but could not have been its cause.

The worsening climatic conditions, in particular repeated low Niles, would have been a serious blow to Egypt's economy and would have caused considerable hardship at any time. The area of fields under cultivation diminished, the size of the harvest decreased, and the numbers of livestock were reduced. Yet it is difficult to accept even this as the single decisive factor which would have brought the Old Kingdom down. The changes were taking place slowly over a period of years. A well-functioning state would have been able to alleviate the worst consequences of natural disasters and organize countermeasures. It is hard to imagine that an administration which was capable of organizing projects such as pyramid-building would not have been able to instigate further intensive reclamation of land in the Delta, the Faiyum, or to inaugurate irrigation programmes in other areas.

What was it, then, that caused the first Egyptian civilization to disintegrate? Was the collapse which ensued inevitable? The seeds of the decline of the Old Kingdom were already present at its birth, and the dynamics of the process were contained in the system itself. The gradual shift in the ownership of land from the central authority to cult and temple establishments, as well as to private tomb endowments, was undermining the very foundations on which the state stood. These changes were not affecting agricultural production, but, by weakening the royal authority, they were slowly preparing conditions for a return to a situation comparable to that before the creation of one state. The consequences of this policy caused irreparable damage to state ideology because its chief representative could no longer live up to its expectations. This in turn made the state economy, in particular its system of official ('ex-officio') property which was now being transformed into private property, unworkable. There was no repressive apparatus effectively available to the king to enforce its continuation.

The eventual disintegration of the political structure which emerged at the beginning of the Third Dynasty from the chrysalis of the Predynastic Period and the first dynasties, was then unavoidable. Pepy II's long reign contributed to the decline, and Egypt's inability to maintain its influence outside its borders was a symptom of the malaise. The worsening of climatic conditions, unfortunately, came at a time when Egyptian administration was no longer in a position to react, and so it delivered the decisive blow. Without such intervention, Egypt would probably have gradually transformed into a conglomeration of smaller territorial entities. In the absence of foreign interference, these could have existed reasonably prosperously until inner pressures built up within society to such an extent that a new political solution was required. This would not necessarily have led to the type of state which eventually emerged as the Egyptian Middle Kingdom. Unfortunately, this was not to be. When new moves towards political unity appeared during the First Intermediate Period, it was, inevitably, again the Old Kingdom pattern which was sought and imitated.

TEN

EPILOGUE

THE OLD KINGDOM EXPERIENCE left an indelible mark upon Egyptian consciousness and found its expression in pessimistic literature whose theme was the futility of worldly pursuits. In the Middle Kingdom text known as *The Man Who Tired of Life*, the soul (*ba*) says to man: 'The builders in granite, those who erected halls in beautiful pyramids in fine work—when the builders become gods, their offering-tables are destroyed as if they were the weary-ones who are dead on the river bank for lack of a rescuer.' Spiritual achievements may make man's name live longer than his material provisions for afterlife. The song of a harpist in the Eleventh Dynasty tomb of Intef made a similar point: 'The gods of the past rest in their pyramids, the blessed nobles likewise are buried in their tombs, but the cult-places of the builders of mansions are gone. What has become of them? I have heard the words of Imhotep and Hardedef recited as their sayings in full. Yet what about their cult-places? Their walls have crumbled, their cult-places are gone as if they had never been.' These are signs of a profound ideological crisis which must have shaken Egypt's very foundations.

Even though many of the features of Old Kingdom administration, religion, literature, arts, and architecture, were eagerly studied and copied in later times, in reality there was no way back. Egypt had new periods of prosperity yet to come, but like a child suddenly matured by a harrowing experience, it could never regain the same self-assurance and blind confidence in its own resources and abilities displayed earlier. The times had changed and new forces appeared which made sure that the old economic and political model could not be resurrected. Old Kingdom pyramids and temples became things of the past, only to be visited and admired. A graffito at Saqqara records such a visit: 'The scribe Ahmose, son of Yeptah, came to see the temple of Djoser. He found it as though heaven were within it, with the sun rising in it, and he said: Let bread, oxen, fowl, and all good and pure things be given to the spirit of the justified Djoser, may heaven rain fresh myrrh, may it drip incense.'

The star-covered ceiling of the interior of the pyramid of Teti at Saqqara. To become an 'indestructible star' was one of the king's aspirations in afterlife.

More than any other Egyptian monuments, the Giza pyramids of the three famous kings of the Fourth Dynasty never ceased to fire people's imagination. Their burial chambers had almost certainly already been plundered during the period of chaos and disorder which followed the end of the Old Kingdom. Some attempts were made to restore at least their interiors and contents during the Ramessid and Late Periods.

CHRONOLOGICAL TABLE

As no safely astronomically fixed dates are available from Egypt during the 3rd millennium BC, absolute chronology (i.e. in years BC) can still be subject to corrections. These might be of the order of some 150 years for the first two dynasties (and more for the Predynastic Period), and up to some 50 years for the Old Kingdom. Relative chronology (i.e. the order of kings) is, with one or two minor exceptions, secure.

In the Old Kingdom the king had five names. The oldest, the Horus-name, was usually written in a *serekh* ('palace façade'), and is given here for the kings of the first three dynasties whenever possible. The kings of the Fourth to Sixth Dynasties are listed by both their *ni-sut-bit* ('prenomen') and the 'son of Re' (birth name or 'nomen') names when these are different. They used to be written in cartouches (oval frames). The names of the kings of the Seventh and Eighth Dynasties are quoted, except for those indicated by ★, in the form in which they appear in the Abdju (Abydos) king-list.

PREDYNASTIC PERIOD	*c.* 5000/4500–2925 BC
united Egypt	at least as early as 2950 BC
Narmer (probably same as King 'Scorpion')	*c.* 2950–2925 BC

FIRST AND SECOND DYNASTIES	*c.* 2925–2658 BC

FIRST DYNASTY:
Aha (Teti of Abdju king-list, Athothis of Manetho)
Djer
Djet
Den
Andjib
Semerkhet
Qaa

SECOND DYNASTY:
Hetepsekhemui
Raneb
Ninetjer
Weneg (*ni-sut-bit* name)
Send (*ni-sut-bit* name)
Sneferka
Sekhemib-perenmaet, perhaps same as Peribsen (= 'Seth-name')
Khasekhem, perhaps same as Khasekhemui-nebuihetepimef (= 'Horus-and-Seth name')

THE OLD KINGDOM (THIRD TO EIGHTH DYNASTIES)	2658–2135 BC
THIRD DYNASTY	2658–2584 BC
Zanakht (*ni-sut-bit* Nebka, Manetho's Nekherophes)	2658–2639 BC
Netjerikhet (Djoser of later tradition)	2639–2620 BC
Sekhemkhet	2620–2614 BC
Khaba	2614–2608 BC
Qahedjet	2608–2584 BC
FOURTH DYNASTY	2584–2465 BC
Snofru	2584–2560 BC
Khufu	2560–2537 BC
Radjedef	2537–2529 BC
Khephren	2529–2504 BC
Khnemka or Wehemka (reading uncertain)	2504–2499 BC
Menkaure	2499–2471 BC
Shepseskaf	2471–2467 BC
Thamphthis (name only known from Manetho)	2467–2465 BC

FIFTH DYNASTY	2465–2322 BC
Userkaf	2465–2458 BC
Sahure	2458–2446 BC
Neferirkare Kakai	2446–2436 BC
Shepseskare	2436–2429 BC
Raneferef (= Izi?)	2429–2419 BC
Neuserre Iny	2419–2388 BC
Menkauhor (also Ikauhor)	2388–2380 BC
Djedkare Izezi	2380–2352 BC
Unas	2352–2322 BC
SIXTH DYNASTY	2322–2151 BC
Teti	2322–2292 BC
Meryre (Neferzahor) Pepy I	2291–2254 BC
Merenre I Nemtyemzaf	2253–2248 BC
Neferkare Pepy II	2247–2154 BC
Merenre-Nemtyemzaf II (from Abdju king-list)	2153–2152 BC
Neitiqert	2152–2151 BC
SEVENTH DYNASTY	2151–2145 BC

Netjerkare
Menkare
Neferkare★
Neferkare-neby
Djedkare-shema
Neferkare-khendu
Merenhor
Neferka-min
Nikare
Neferkare-terer
Neferkahor

EIGHTH DYNASTY	2145–2135 BC

Neferkare-pepysonb
Neferka-min-anu
Qakare Ibi★
Neferkaure
Neferkauhor
Neferirkare

The period which follows, 2134–2040 BC, is known as the First Intermediate Period, and is succeeded by the Middle Kingdom.

BIBLIOGRAPHY

The list contains selected monographs and larger works dealing with various aspects of the Old Kingdom and the preceding period. Much of the discussion concerning some of the topics covered in this book has been conducted on pages of specialized journals, not readily accessible to non-specialists. References to such articles have been omitted here, but the works cited below include them in their own bibliographies.

The main source for hieroglyphic texts of the Old Kingdom still remains Kurt Sethe's *Urkunden des Alten Reichs*, 2nd ed. Leipzig 1933, even though many new inscriptions have become known since its publication. For references to Old Kingdom material from the Memphite area see B. Porter, R. L. B. Moss, E. W. Burney, and J. Malek, *Topographical Bibliography of Ancient Egyptian Hieroglyphic Texts, Reliefs, and Paintings*, III, 2nd ed. in 2 vols., Griffith Institute, Ashmolean Museum, Oxford 1974 and 1981. It also lists references to excavation reports and publications of material not included in our Bibliography.

ALDRED, Cyril *Egypt to the End of the Old Kingdom* (Thames and Hudson, London 1965)

ARKELL, A. J. *The Prehistory of the Nile Valley* (Handbuch der Orientalistik, 7.1.2A.1, E. J. Brill, Leiden/Köln 1975)

ATZLER, Michael *Untersuchungen zur Herausbildung von Herrschaftsformen in Ägypten* Hildesheimer Ägyptologische Beiträge, 16, Gerstenberg Verlag, Hildesheim 1981)

BAUMGARTEL, Elise J. *The Cultures of Prehistoric Egypt*, 2 vols. (Griffith Institute, Ashmolean Museum, Oxford 1955 and 1960)

BAUMGARTEL, Elise J. *Predynastic Egypt* (Chapter IXa of *CAH³* i, Pt. 1, Cambridge University Press 1970, pp.463–97)

BAER, Klaus *Rank and Title in the Old Kingdom. The Structure of the Egyptian Administration in the Fifth and Sixth Dynasties* (The University of Chicago Press 1960)

BEGELSBACHER-FISCHER, Barbara L. *Untersuchungen zur Götterwelt des Alten Reiches im Spiegel der Privatgräber der IV. und V. Dynastie* (Orbis Biblicus et Orientalis, 37, Universitätsverlag Freiburg, Schweiz/Vandenhoeck & Ruprecht, Göttingen 1981)

BUTZER, Karl W. *Early Hydraulic Civilization in Egypt. A Study in Cultural Ecology* (Prehistoric Archaeology and Ecology, The University of Chicago Press, Chicago and London 1976)

EDWARDS, I. E. S. *The Early Dynastic Period in Egypt* (Chapter XI of *CAH³* i, Pt. 2, Cambridge University Press 1971, pp.1–70)

EDWARDS, I. E. S. *The Pyramids of Egypt* (Penguin Books, Harmondsworth 1985)

EMERY, Walter B. *Archaic Egypt* (Penguin Books, Harmondsworth 1961)

FAKHRY, Ahmed *The Pyramids* (The University of Chicago Press, Chicago and London, 2nd ed. 1969)

GOEDICKE, Hans *Königliche Dokumente aus dem Alten Reich* (Ägyptologische Abhandlungen, 14, Otto Harrassowitz, Wiesbaden 1967)

GOEDICKE, Hans *Die privaten Rechtsinschriften aus dem Alten Reich* (Beihefte zur Wiener Zeitschrift für die Kunde des Morgenlandes, 5, Verlag Notring, Wien 1970)

GOEDICKE, Hans *Die Stellung des Königs im Alten Reich* (Ägyptologische Abhandlungen, 2, Otto Harrassowitz, Wiesbaden 1960)

HAYES, William C. (ed. by SEELE, Keith C.) *Most Ancient Egypt* (The University of Chicago Press, Chicago & London 1965)

HELCK, Wolfgang *Die Beziehungen Ägyptens zu Vorderasien im 3. und 2. Jahrtausend v. Chr.* (Ägyptologische Abhandlungen, 5, Otto Harrassowitz, Wiesbaden, 2nd ed. 1971)

HELCK, Wolfgang *Geschichte des Alten Ägypten* (Handbuch der Orientalistik, 1.1.3, E. J. Brill, Leiden/Köln 1968)

HELCK, Wolfgang *Untersuchungen zu den Beamtentiteln des ägyptischen Alten Reiches* (Ägyptologische Forschungen, 18, Verlag J. J. Augustin, Glückstadt–Hamburg–New York 1954)

HELCK, Wolfgang *Untersuchungen zu Manetho und den ägyptischen Königslisten* (Untersuchungen zur Geschichte und Altertumskunde Aegyptens, 18, Akademie-Verlag, Berlin 1956)

HELCK, Wolfgang *Wirtschaftsgeschichte des Alten Ägypten im 3. und 2. Jahrtausend vor Chr.* (Handbuch der Orientalistik, 1.1.5, E. J. Brill, Leiden/Köln 1975)

HOFFMAN, Michael A. *Egypt before the Pharaohs. The Prehistoric Foundations of Egyptian Civilization* (Routledge & Kegan Paul, London & Henley 1980)

JACQUET-GORDON, Helen K. *Les noms des domaines funéraires sous l'Ancien Empire égyptien* (Bibliothèque d'Étude, XXXIV, I.F.A.O., 1962)

KANAWATI, Naguib *The Egyptian Administration in The Old Kingdom. Evidence on its Economic Decline* (Aris & Phillips Ltd., Warminster 1977)

KANAWATI, Naguib *Governmental Reforms in Old Kingdom Egypt* (Modern Egyptology, Aris & Phillips Ltd., Warminster 1980)

KEMP, Barry J. *Old Kingdom, Middle Kingdom and Second Intermediate Period c. 2686–1552 BC* (Chapter 2 of TRIGGER, B. G.; KEMP, B. J.; O'CONNOR, D. and LLOYD, A. B. *Ancient Egypt. A Social History*, Cambridge University Press 1983, pp.71–182)

LAUER, Jean-Philippe *Histoire monumentale des pyramides d'Égypte*, i. *Les pyramides à degrés (IIIᵉ Dynastie)* (Bibliothèque d'Étude, XXXIX, I.F.A.O., Cairo 1962)

LAUER, Jean-Philippe *Le mystère des pyramides* (Presses de la Cité, Paris 1974)

MARTIN-PARDEY, Eva *Untersuchungen zur ägyptischen Provinzialverwaltung bis zum Ende des Alten Reiches* (Hildesheimer Ägyptologische Beiträge, 1, Verlag Gebrüder Gerstenberg, Hildesheim 1976)

MRSICH, Tycho *Untersuchungen zur Hausurkunde des Alten Reiches. Ein Beitrag zum altägyptischen Stiftungsrecht* (Münchner Ägyptologische Studien, 13, Verlag Bruno Hessling, Berlin 1968)

POSENER-KRIÉGER, Paule *Les archives du temple funéraire de Néferirkarê-Kakaï (Les Papyrus d'Abousir). Traduction et commentaire*, 2 vols. (Bibliothèque d'Étude, LXV, I.F.A.O., Cairo 1976)

RANSOM WILLIAMS, Caroline *The Decoration of the Tomb of Per-ñeb. The Technique and the Color Conventions* (The Metropolitan Museum of Art, New York 1932)

SCHENKEL, Wolfgang *Die Bewässerungsrevolution im Alten Ägypten* (D.A.I. Abteilung Kairo, Verlag Philipp von Zabern, Mainz/Rhein 1978)

SMITH, William Stevenson (revised with additions by SIMPSON, William Kelly) *The Art and Architecture of Ancient Egypt* (Penguin Books, Harmondsworth 1981)

SMITH, William Stevenson *A History of Egyptian Sculpture and Painting in the Old Kingdom* (The Museum of Fine Arts, Boston, 2nd ed. 1949)

SMITH, William Stevenson *The Old Kingdom in Egypt and the Beginning of the First Intermediate Period* (Chapter XIV of *CAH³* i, Pt. 2, Cambridge University Press 1971, pp.145–207)

TRIGGER, B. G. *The Rise of Egyptian Civilization* (Chapter I of TRIGGER, B. G.; KEMP, B. J.; O'CONNOR, D. and LLOYD, A. B. *Ancient Egypt. A Social History*, Cambridge University Press 1983, pp.1–70)

ZIBELIUS, Karola *Ägyptische Siedlungen nach Texten des Alten Reiches* (Beihefte zum Tübinger Atlas des Vorderen Orients, Reihe B[Geisteswissenschaften], 19, Dr. Ludwig Reichert Verlag, Wiesbaden 1978)

The sources of the quotations at the beginnings of the Chapters are as follows: p. 7, the name of the pyramid of Pepy I at southern Saqqara; p. 14, a Fifth Dynasty text endowing a tomb at Giza, now in Cairo, Egyptian Museum, CG 1432; p. 18, Papyrus Prisse, 88–9; p. 22, Pyramid Texts, §272; p. 25, artist's signature alongside the staff held by the official Djau in his late Sixth Dynasty tomb at Deir el-Gebrawi; p. 26, Papyrus Leiden 344 *recto*, 2,11.

INDEX

ACKNOWLEDGMENTS

Werner Forman and the publishers would like to acknowledge
the help of the following museums in permitting the photography
shown on the pages listed:
The British Museum: 18 below, 23 below, 27, 86, 113 top. The
    Ashmolean Museum, Oxford: 16, 17, 18 top, 19, 20, 21, 22,
    24, 25, 28, 29, 30, 33 left, 36, 37. The Louvre, Paris: 8, 34, 121.
    The Egyptian Museum, Cairo: 9, 14–15, 32, 33 right, 35, 38,
    54, 55, 58, 61, 62, 63, 71, 78, 82, 83, 88–89, 90–91, 92, 94–95,
    98, 99, 102, 110, 112, 113 bottom, 115 bottom.

Werner Forman would also like to thank the following for their
help:
T. G. H. James and Dr A. H. Spencer, British Museum; Dr
    Mohamed Saleh, Egyptian Museum; Dr Wafaa Taha El
    Sadeek, Cairo; Dr Helen Whitehouse, Ashmolean Museum;
    Nassif Hassan, Dr Ahmed Kadry, Dr Mohamed Ibrahim Aly,
    Cairo; Mme C. Belanger, Mlle Harlé, Mlle Delange, Jean-
    Louis Hellouin de Cenival, Louvre.

Jaromir Malek wishes to thank Dr Graham Piddock for the
translation of the passage from Herodotus, Book II, 35–6, quoted
in the Prologue. He would also like to use this opportunity to
express his appreciation of the help received from the staff of the
Ashmolean Library (Griffith Institute), Oxford.